How to Be a Great Single Dad

How to be a Great Single Dad

Theo Theobald

Hay House
Australia • Canada • Hong Kong
South Africa • United Kingdom • United States

Published and distributed in the United Kingdom by Hay House UK Ltd,
Unit 62, Canalot Studios, 222 Kensal Rd, London W10 5BN. Tel.: (44) 20
8962 1230; Fax: (44) 20 8962 1239. www.hayhouse.co.uk

Published and distributed in Australia by Hay House Australia Ltd, 18/36
Ralph St, Alexandria NSW 2015. Tel.: (61) 2 9669 4299; Fax: (61) 2 9669
4144. www.hayhouse.com.au

Published and distributed in the Republic of South Africa by Hay House
SA (Pty), Ltd, PO Box 990, Witkoppen 2068. Tel./Fax: (27) 11 706 6612.
orders@psdprom.co.za

Distributed in Canada by Raincoast, 9050 Shaughnessy St, Vancouver,
BC V6P 6E5. Tel.: (1) 604 323 7100; Fax: (1) 604 323 2600

A catalogue record for this book is available from the British Library.

ISBN 1-4019-0694-X

Composition by Scribe Design Ltd, Ashford, Kent, UK
Printed and bound in Great Britain by TJ International Ltd, Padstow,
Cornwall

For Ben and Nancy...
...who else

contents

Introduction

I've only got one qualification for writing this. I am a single dad.

I don't pretend for a minute to be great at it. There are days when I am (by accident perhaps) but I reckon there are just as many when I'm not. The important thing is I *aspire* to be great and I think I know what greatness is, partly from the feedback from my own children but just as much in the observation of lots of others with their dads.

I'm not a behavioural psychologist (whatever that is), a schoolteacher, dietitian, paediatrician or a trained counsellor. I'm just an ordinary bloke, like lots of others, trying to get it right for my kids and myself, in the certain knowledge that we'll always think we could have done better.

I hope that most of the content is familiar territory and you can relate easily to it, because I found that there are just too many books, written by people (both men and women) who are trying to work their way through their own personal break-up. The result is introspective and dull and just makes me feel that there's someone out there who *thinks* they're worse off than we are.

I'm also assuming that you've already split up and are not reading this in anticipation. In the early chapters I talk about how hard the breakdown of relationships can be, but I'm certain that 'staying together for the children' is a flawed plan. I have this on the authority of a good friend whose parents did just that and she wishes they'd had the courage to end it, rather than make her childhood miserable with their rowing and stand-offs. I think it's equally true that there is no good time to split up as far as the children are concerned; they will always be devastated whatever their age, it's just that it will manifest itself in different ways according to the maturity of their emotions.

With rising divorce rates, loads of us are ending up in funny, mismatched families, mum and dad taking it in turns to cope on their own; one parent, or both in new relationships; sometimes extra kids from former liaisons chucked in for good measure. I couldn't cover every eventuality, so if *your* circumstances are different to mine I hope that there's still enough common sense in these pages for you to take the bit that applies to you.

It won't surprise you though that lots of the examples I quote have either happened to me, or I could have imagined they would, but I've tried to jumble them up with stories from my other contributors (lots of other blokes in the same situation as me), partly to present a broader range of experiences, but also because I don't need to share, and you don't need to know, the details of my break-up. If you're into that kind of voyeurism, then I'd recommend EastEnders instead.

Now and again you will find a specific reference to my son (now aged 12) and daughter (10, going on 15); because they have been at the heart of my learning experience over the last few years and also because I'm proud enough of them to want to give them some credit for my writing this. Without them, I wouldn't have been a dad of any description and how sad would that be?

The last thing I set out to do was create an instruction manual. All kids are different and so are all dads, but there have been plenty of times when I've wondered if it was only me who felt a particular way about an issue and it would have been good to know that someone else did too. But this book isn't about my break-up, or yours, it's about moving on from where we are and making the very best of the situation we're now faced with.

You'll see from the examples that most of the experience I've drawn is from fathers who still have some hands-on responsibility for their children's upbringing, so we're looking at an age group from infancy through to late teens. That's not to say that being a good dad ends there, but as they reach maturity (about 14 in their eyes, 44 in yours), their care needs will doubtless get less pastoral and become more financial.

I very much subscribe to the theory that from the moment our children are born we are charged with the task of helping them grow away from us a little more every day; we teach them how to become independent of us, it's our job. Indeed, by the time the late teen phase is reached, we should have already been a distinct embarrassment to them for many years.

More than anything, I hope this book helps you by supporting your natural 'dad skills', to the point where someday, after the close nurturing phase has run its course, they'll come back to you, full of admiration and completely convinced of the fact that in bringing them up, you did your best.

A matter of circumstance

There are lots of ways we can be single dads, my own circumstances are that I got divorced about five years ago. After some initial stupidity and shenanigans (on both sides) we agreed that our two children should live with their mum for most of the time, but come and stay with me on alternate weekends, and that I would have them for half of the school holidays.

I live close by (on purpose), which means that now I see them, albeit briefly, at least a couple of nights a week and I have them for the odd additional overnight if circumstances allow or dictate.

That said, I recognise this is not the case for everyone. For you, access to your children may be more limited, perhaps by circumstances (you live a long way away) or possibly because you've not been able to agree a suitable level of contact which everyone is happy with. I can only imagine how difficult that might be and if you're faced with that scenario, you have my sympathy and doubtless that of all the other single dads who have managed to get themselves 'sorted' in a more satisfactory way.

On the other hand, you might be one of the unusual (and in my book saintly) blokes who have custody of the children, so they're with you most of the time and visit mum's place on some kind of agreed basis. I can only guess that this must be very different, sometimes even a burden, as you have to take much more responsibility for their day-to-day well-being. My guess is that for all I miss my children when they're not with me (and that doesn't diminish over time), you have much the tougher deal, as indeed do many single mums.

Finally, the even tougher set of circumstances is where you are a widower and you not only are deprived of the 'relief' of getting some time to yourself when the children are away, but also have to cope with being full-time mum *and* dad to them.

I hope that these few paragraphs don't seem like just a passing reference to the many dads whose situation I don't share, or to make it seem like I am trivialising just how hard life can be for them, but I can only really explain to you the way the world looks from where I and the majority of other single dads are standing. If at times it appears that I don't understand what it's like for you, then you are probably right, I can only apologise and hope that no matter what your individual personal circumstances are, you will find some common sense and solace in what I've written.

Book structure

If you want to you can read this book from cover to cover in the conventional way. However, because of where you're up to in your personal life and based on your current knowledge of the skills of fatherhood, you might prefer to dip into the sections that suit you at the time you need them. Here's a quick run down to help you navigate.

Section I

This is about the break-up of relationships and the immediate period afterwards. It's not by any stretch of the imagination a bag of laughs but any of us who have been through it know that can never be the case. Hopefully though, it will give you a bit of insight into how it's been for other blokes (me included) and in the midst of the stresses and strains you might pick up the kind of advice I wish I'd had, just because it might have made the kids' lives easier. You may gather from this that, like lots of single dads, I have regrets about the way I handled some of the issues around the break-up and if I could help anyone to reduce their chances of making the same mistakes, I would.

Section II

This is far cheerier. It's also a lot longer because it really forms the core of the 'How to' part of the book, which is what I promised you in the title. Apart from a great load of tips on how to be a modern housekeeper and keep your place spick and span (well, as much as you'd want to), there is far more exciting stuff like how to plan great holidays, and a ton of advice on keeping kids entertained (with the specific objective that you too will get pleasure from it).

You'll also find out how and where to buy suitable clothes for your kids, as well as solving that problem we all suffer from, remembering all the essential dates for kids like school holidays, birthdays and even Hallowe'en!

Section III

This is all about learning. Apart from being involved in the formal education system, there are lots of other lessons we can help our children with, including some life learning and a set of values to bring them up with that'll make you proud of them every day. You might also discover a thing or two yourself in the chapter entitled 'Sex and drugs and rock and roll'!

Section IV

This focuses on the tricky area of behaviour and contains advice about where to set the boundaries, how much discipline to apply and when. It might also help you to understand the kind of behaviour that children like to see *us* display, so you'll find lots of sound advice on how to be great in their eyes.

Section V

This is really about you and your future. However well you are doing as a single dad, you also need to see yourself as an individual and my firm belief is that the children's happiness is very much dictated by yours. It seems appropriate then to spend some time looking at what will make you happy in the future, including the possibility of a new relationship.

Before you embark on the rest of the text, I need to tell you about one of the fundamental mistakes that I kept repeating until quite recently. When I didn't know the answer to some question of parenting, I felt hopelessly inadequate, as if I should have been able to refer to some inner paternal muse who would offer me a range of instant solutions. Lots of people have said to me that there's no manual for parenting, we all just do what we can in the hope that it's right most of the time, and just because we're faced with the job of lone parenting I can't see any reason why that would change.

I now think it's quite normal not to know the answer in every situation and because of that I'm much more at ease calling on outside sources of enlightenment, which could be friends, family, even the doctor or a religious or spiritual leader – they've all got a valid point of view.

Beyond all that, you've still got you and one of the key things I've learned is that your two most reliable parenting allies are instinct and common sense.

BREAK-UP AND AFTERMATH

1

I wouldn't start from here if I were you

Break-ups hurt. They really hurt.

There's just about no one who gets off scot-free either. Even if you've endured many miserable years in a relationship that didn't work on any level, I defy you to walk away without an occasional wistful look back at how it *might* have been. This is because all of us enter into relationships with hope for a happy future, so when it doesn't come about, we feel let down, sometimes by the other party, sometimes by ourselves, often both. If I'm honest I could really have done without writing this chapter – after all, why would I relish going back to such a painful time in my own life? But I know that to end up a single dad you have to face the 'loss' of your partner, and how you cope in the early days can be critically important for the kids. Personally, despite how awful it was, I found it to be one of the most enlightening periods of self-discovery I've ever been through, not least because I had to think hard about what I really wanted out of life for me and for my children.

So, reluctant though I may be to embark on this part of the journey, I see no alternative. I hope that what I learned helps you understand that this phase doesn't last too long and life gets better when it's over.

When a break-up first happens, it can be like bereavement – there is a series of moods we all go through, not necessarily in sequence, but more on a random spin of the emotional wheel. Although this is different for each of us, it can seem like the wheel is spinning hopelessly out of control, with mood swings that change minute by minute, fuelled by people around us or our own self-pity, or triggered by something as simple as spotting the particular brand of bath cleaner she used to buy, on a supermarket shelf (and they say men aren't romantic!). Different blokes in diverse circumstances described to me some of the following feelings, so have a look, in a bit more detail, at some of the moods below and see if they ring a bell:

- **Remorse** 'How did I end up in this sorry state? I was so full of hope for the future, so wanted it to all work out (in a movie-love kind of way). How innocent I was and in retrospect, how foolish. If only ... if only ...'

- **Anger** 'Bloody, flipping, blinking bitch! How could she? I gave her the best years of my life and what do I get in return? Well?... Hmmm, well, I'm going to show you, missy. I'm going to show you ... errm, well, I'm not sure exactly what but believe me, one day, I am going to show you ... *something*.'

- **Indifference** 'Frankly, my dear, I don't give a damn! You're confusing me with someone who gives a toss ... You live your life and I'll live mine, just don't come round here trying to tell me what I should do next, not now, not ever, not never, no way.'

- **Jealousy** 'Fine! You get it all, don't you? The lifestyle, the new romance, the money, the friends, the cat, the kids – well, don't you worry about me, will you?'

- **Bitterness** 'Good bloody riddance, that's what I say. I'm clearing out all your junk, chucking away all those rubbish CDs you bought me and those stupid novelty underpants you thought were so hilarious every Christmas.'

It's easy when all this is happening to mix your emotions up with those of the kids, but you need to recognise that what they're going through is different. Do your best to keep these things separate and don't try to get them to say it's all OK for them if it's not.

Of course, where you are up to in your own head and the number of different mood swings you go through will be dependent on the circumstances surrounding your individual break-up, but if you're finding your emotions hard to keep under control it's worth bearing in mind that there are external factors which will help or hinder your recovery. Here are a few of them to be thinking about.

People close to you, like friends and family, can be a great source of comfort. Equally, they can cause you more grief by expressing their opinions, questioning you on what went wrong in the past or quizzing you on your future. They're only trying to help but sometimes it's hard to see that at the time. The one that's bound to get to you is when they say they 'never liked her' and couldn't understand how you ended up together – this is made all the worse because you know *her* lot are saying exactly the same about you right now. It's a bit like moaning about family; *you* can say what you like to your mate in the pub about how your sister drives you demented, or your mum makes you mad, but if *they* offer any personal criticism of your kith and kin, you (illogically) jump to their defence. Even the most vitriolic of fallouts with an ex-spouse can still leave you with the dregs of loyalty. Maybe the biggest factor is not the criticism they might level at your ex but the implied failings that you have shown, in either choosing her, putting up with her or not noticing when she was sleeping with your brother.

Work too can make things better or worse. If you have a busy job, it can be a way of forgetting about the emotional things and just getting on with what has to be done. Outsiders are sometimes surprised that people who are going through a break-up work harder and more efficiently than at other times, but it can be a way of asserting ourselves again and re-building some of the self-esteem we might have lost in other areas of our lives. It might be that we've been wedded to our work for some time – a relationship our former wife may have seen as bigamous – and that it has directly or otherwise been part of the reason for the split. Just as with a fresh new relationship we might find ourselves spending more time than ever in strengthening the bond between us. The big danger here is in putting all your eggs in one basket, as now is the time when you need to broaden the base of your self-worth and support network, if you're going to 'recover' in the shortest possible time. Just as work can be a welcome distraction from the emotional hassle you're having to deal with outside, it can also add to the stress you are having to cope with elsewhere – just try to be aware of how you are feeling inside and the extra burden being carried by your emotional self.

There is a whole load of what I'd call 'artificial crutches' you can rely on as well. If you really are feeling the strain, go and see your doctor. Don't do that bloke thing, 'Oh, it's OK, I can cope' (so often said by men with veins bulging from their foreheads and steam emanating from their ears). If you leave asking for help too late, you might find that there's nothing very macho about a nervous breakdown.

I'm glad that, in general, attitudes do seem to have changed in this area and I think that recognising that we can get *emotionally* sick, as well as physically, is a positive step towards self-preservation. There's no shame in taking what's prescribed; for the time being, it's about what gets you through the night. If you've got a cold, you take all sorts of stuff to ease the symptoms but none of it actually makes you better, it's you – your system – that does that. The linctus just helps you forget you're feeling rough (and if you take enough helps you forget your own name), it's your immune system that repairs the damage. The 'emotional sickness' that we all suffer from sometimes is exactly the same. You don't have to grin and bear it though, you can take something (your doctor will know what) to ease the pain until your ability to self-repair kicks in.

In today's society, there is a plentiful supply of other substances that can do the same thing, the most common being alcohol, and while I don't want to get preachy about all this, I think it's a good idea to check yourself now and again and think about your intake. It's really hard to be a great dad if you're out of it all the time. If you're worried that alcohol or other substances are becoming an issue for you, the same advice applies as above: you should visit your GP (and not because he can prescribe it on the NHS).

All these things can be forces of good or evil, as you bounce around the pinball table of emotion. Eventually, all this passes and most blokes I've spoken to say two things. Firstly, that when you look back it all seems a bit hazy, like you were just going through the motions, and secondly, we all spent too long in recovery and should have shaken ourselves out of it sooner. The fact that I've noticed this will not dramatically alter anyone's future because, as we all know, hindsight is a wonderful thing. The best you can hope to do is to cut down the amount of time you spend in 'emotional rehab'; it's not a pretty sight.

In the midst of this emotional maelstrom, you might be forgiven for making the odd error of judgement in front of the children, so try to be aware of the following four chaps, all of whom we risk behaving like.

Mr Vengeful

He says things like 'Well, that's typical of your mother' but it's as much the way he says it that upsets the children. They may be old enough to understand you've fallen out but they still love both of you and they don't want to be forced into a position where they have to side with one or the other. If you do hate her with a vengeance at the moment, then talk to your mates, not your kids. If you really are the wronged party in all of this and have been treated unspeakably badly, then remember that in the long term preserving your dignity gives you the highest of moral high ground. It may be that your kids never realise (or at least admit) that mum was wrong and you were right, so you just have to accept that this may be the case. On the other hand, they do have an uncanny way of arriving at correct conclusions about you both. There must have been times when you were frightened by not only their honesty but also their accuracy ('Dad, you can be such a fusspot sometimes ...'). If you think that some of this typifies where you are now, then be careful because once war has broken out between you, you need to exercise some caution over which battles you choose to fight or the kids will get caught in the crossfire. Stop and think for a minute how important clothes, treats, bedtime, discipline and a host of other things are – yes, they are significant but not more so than the emotional welfare of the children. The truth of most split-ups is that you are both to blame in one way or another and in adulthood the children will look back and realise this. The point-scoring in the early stages doesn't really do anyone any favours, so try to keep it to a minimum.

Mr Indifferent

He's so wrapped up in himself, he really doesn't care what's going on around him at the moment. Exactly what you say to the children about the break-up will vary according to your individual circumstances but whatever it is, you should be prepared to keep talking and listening, at times of their choosing, not yours. The same rules as above apply – just because you've switched off your feelings for your former other half (or they've dwindled away to nothing over a long period), the children will doubtless be more loyal. Often they don't see a relationship degenerating, so it's much harder for them to understand how you 'loved each other yesterday but not today'.

Mr Maudlin

Getting upset in front of the kids doesn't help anyone because they'll just get upset too. You really do have to put a brave face on it here, even in the light of fresh revelations about mum's new private life – it's a bit like in *Tom and Jerry*, where Tom gets thwacked, but has to keep quiet (to avoid waking the dog's son), sometimes you have to go outside to scream. I'm not saying it's wrong to be affected by what you're going through but focus on the kids and you'll see that they've got some shit to put up with too, so the last thing they need is you making it worse. If they've only got 'visiting rights' to your place, it's not too much to expect that you'll save the hand-wringing and teeth-gnashing for the bits in between when you're in the pub with a trusted friend (no doubt testing the strength of that friendship).

Mr Indulgent

I'm waiting for the day (which must come soon) when a sparkly-smiled, suntanned presenter comes on a TV advert and says, 'Got a problem? Then solve it with money ...' because we're increasingly being led to believe that all the bad things in life will go away if you throw enough cash at them. Being the continual bearer of gifts and giver of treats will not do any good in the long term. What kids really want is to be listened to and loved. I'm conscious of banging on about this elsewhere in the book, but it's just so obvious that I'm astounded some people can't see it. Take a look at any of these intrusive TV shows that have a fly-on-the-wall look at dysfunctional families (and, be honest, why would we want to watch a 'functional' one?), and you'll see this mistake being played out time and time again. They say that these days we're 'cash-rich' and 'time-poor'; that's a shame really because all the kids really want is time (oh, and a new games console – only kidding).

All these fellas are pretty unpleasant, even more so if you're their child. I've put them in because there is a balance to be struck between talking to your kids about the break-up and shielding them from some of the grown-up crap that they rightly shouldn't have to deal with. When they're older they may want to know more of what went on but for now it's better if you treat it as X-rated.

Ten things to aid your recovery

So, you're moody about the break-up, have a ton of other issues to deal with, some of which are positive but others are not and you risk slipping into the personality of one of our stereotypes above. Man, do you need help!

This isn't a cure-all that will make all the nastiness go away but here's a list of things that you might choose to do in order to banish some of the worst behaviours you might be otherwise tempted into. In the main they're innocent pleasures and are by no means an exhaustive collection. There are hundreds of ways you can make yourself feel better and if none of these suits you, then I hope they spark your thinking into coming up with your own innocent indulgences.

Join a gym

Radical, I know, but exercise is great for releasing those endorphin things that are supposed to make us feel happy. (Didn't I read somewhere that chocolate does the same thing? Maybe, but too much will make you fat and spotty, so best avoid it.) If you're not keen on the idea of donning your washed-out baggy shorts and being made to feel like a 'dorky weakling' amongst the Lycra-clad Beautiful People, you might choose something a bit gentler like a brisk walk; alright, a casual saunter, if you prefer. Don't just do it once though or you'll feel like it was a waste of time – come to that, it would be.

Go to college

Or night school, or sign up for a home-learning programme. New skills and new achievements are something we can feel rightly proud of and you don't have to climb Everest to make a substantial shift in the way you feel. I tried a whole variety of things – 'Cooking for Blokes', 'Creative Writing', 'Photoshop' (a computer graphics program). My only disappointment is that they wouldn't let me join the 'Belly-dancing for the Over Fifties' class. Don't you just hate it when you're discriminated against on the grounds of being too young?

Plan a trip

This is especially good if you can involve the kids. Again, it doesn't have to be an assault on the Matterhorn (maybe one too many mountaineering analogies here), it can be as simple as a visit to a museum or circus or the theatre. I bet if you visit your local Tourist Information Office, you'll find tons of things locally that you were only vaguely aware of. If you get the chance, talk to other parents in the locality who have children of a similar age and get some personal recommendations. The Internet is also great for uncovering stuff to do and with so much information about you can match the activity to your budget.

Bake bread

This one might sound a bit 'left field' but there is something therapeutic about it. I think it's to do with that 'Back to Basics' Earth Mother (or in our case Father) ethic. Even the process of kneading the dough is supposed to be soothing (rather than erotic) and when you've finished you can even make yourself a sandwich with the fruits of your labours. Personally, I'd find this a bit strange as a solo activity but it's great fun if you share it with your children; who knows, it may even have the same soothing effect on them. Apparently, John Lennon used to bake bread for exactly this purpose. What is less clear is whether or not he only took it up *after* getting married.

Buy clothes

Be careful! The way you look can do wonders for the way you feel but don't be tempted into a full makeover without some third-party advice. Find your own style guru who will be honest enough to tell you when you look stupid. Remember, the aim of all these activities is to increase your self-esteem, not provide amusement and entertainment for the people who see you walking down the street. The greatest temptation of all is to go young and trendy in the misguided belief that we will look great, be attractive to women and really annoy our ex when she sees just how cool we can be – everybody will just think you're an idiot, including you when you look back in a few years' time. I once worked with a bloke who remodelled himself on George Michael: clothes, facial hair, the lot. What an idiot (see, told you).

Write a letter

A great starting point is to make a list of all the old mates you meant to keep in touch with but never seemed to get round to. You may find that after the split you don't get 'custody' of the friends, so it may be that you'll have to go further back and re-kindle a pre-marital friendship. Before you sit down to spill the beans about how awful your life is, think about the person you're sending it to and *write the sort of stuff they might want to read*. It's a really good idea to ask how they are and what's been happening since you last saw them in 1986. There's something wonderfully soothing about putting your thoughts down on paper – you might discover that life isn't as bad as you believed it was and there might be the added bonus that you receive a reply. Personally, I can't think of anything better than getting post that doesn't include the offer of another credit card or the threat of what will happen to you if you don't pay off the existing one.

Rent a film

Whatever your preferred genre (horror, action/adventure, fantasy sci-fi or just plain fantasy), it may well be that your former squeeze didn't share your taste. Now it doesn't matter because you can make time to sit and wallow in the kind of entertainment that you like (e.g. stopping and rewinding the bit where the Clint says 'Go ahead punk, make my day'). The lift you'll get watching Indiana Jones instead of Bridget Jones (*again*) is really hard to measure. A good wholesome movie that you can lose yourself in is best. I'm rather fond of the old black and white Ealing comedies, or early 'Miss Marple' films with the wonderful Margaret Rutherford. How camp.

Plan a surprise

Again, this is something you can do for the children. It doesn't have to be for a special occasion, or for that matter anything expensive, just something out of the ordinary. I'm tempted to say that everyone loves surprises but I should temper that by warning that they don't always go according to plan – sometimes a sure-fire winner can fall flat, so prepare yourself for that contingency and don't get cross or disappointed if everyone doesn't show universal glee. That said, if you know your kids, you'll get it right most of the time. I once got only a couple of hours with my son on his birthday, not long enough to have a proper party and nowhere to really host it, so instead I picked him up in the 'party car' and drove over to my brother's just to say hello. I filled the inside of my car with balloons, streamers and banners, put 'Happy Birthday' on the stereo and supplied cake and pop for the journey. It went down better than a 'Happy Meal' on a Friday night.

Make a plan

One of the worst things you can do when you're at a low ebb is to simply drift. It wastes time, is counter-productive and stops you feeling better about yourself. As with all these activities, start small – think of modest targets to hit, not life-changing ones. Choose any area of your life and make a decision about how you want to change it, then put in place a realistic timescale, have some thoughts about the milestones along the way and what 'achievement' will look like. Make this an ongoing process and soon you'll find that you've done all sorts of things you never thought possible (apart from 'Belly dancing for the Over Fifties').

Go for a walk

I know you think I've lost the plot and am just repeating the first item on the list but this walk has a different objective from fitness. Seemingly, we have 'no time to stand and stare' but you can make time if you choose. Pick an environment that can be inspirational – the beach, a wooded area or country lane – and just go lose yourself (not literally). You can choose to mull over what's been happening in your life or just appreciate what's around you. Breathe deeply and drink in the beauty of nature; when you realise how small you are in the big picture of the world at large, it's much easier to get a sense of proportion about the bad stuff you face. I headed for the Cornish coast and let the howling wind blow through me as I watched the surf crash against a sea wall. It's such an awesome experience, it's really hard to feel anything but better after it.

You have probably worked out that a lot of these things have something in common – they're deliberately different from the things you used to do. Often you can spot the newly estranged bloke by the too-young-for-his-age hairstyle, the overly-trendy clothes and (heaven help us) the second-hand Ferrari. All of these things are aimed at achieving the same end: a change from what's gone before. I've already cautioned you on the radical makeover but I maintain that the principle of change remains sound – you need to start seeing yourself in a new light, a mild re-invention can do wonders for your self-esteem and it doesn't have to cost the earth. As I said earlier, not all of these things will fit all people; it's more about changing the way you think about yourself than anything else. It's not so much to do with the journey but the destination.

Rebuilding your own self-worth is a vital part to feeling better about the future; and all of this is at a point in your life when you might be struggling emotionally, financially and in a host of other ways. Knowing yourself and under-standing what's going on around you can be a great help. Making some changes can supplement that by giving you back a more positive self-image, but it's not easy.

One of my great failings has always been in wanting to find an instant solution to everything, as if it were some kind of mathematical equation that if you have the right data, the correct formula and enough logical thought, you really can work out what the meaning of life is. If I've learned anything through the process of getting divorced, it is that some things have no answer today, tomorrow or maybe for a long time yet, they take time to work through and, what's more, in some cases there may never be what I'd call a result, only a compromise.

Without doubt this immediate post-break-up phase is when it is really hard to be a great dad, simply because you are having so much trouble convincing yourself that you have any sustainable worth whatever. Sometimes, because of the stresses, you will lose it with the children when it's not their fault, but once things have calmed down again, I think it does no harm to explain and apologise.

One Sunday lunchtime I was being particularly tetchy and bad tempered and although it wasn't their fault, I was taking it out on the children. Eventually, my son snapped and said 'Why are you being so horrible to me?' I barked back 'Because it's my job!', then, calming down a little, I countered with 'Why are you winding me up so much?', and he came right back with 'Because it's mine!' On balance, I'd say he won that one.

So, the good news is that kids can help you get through all of this and give you a reason to like yourself again. How great is that?

2

Solitaire

So, you're single again.

Once the initial trauma of the split has started to subside, there are some issues you'll have to deal with as part of normal life again, albeit a different kind of normality. Usually, this will include times when the children are with you and times when they're not, when you are, in fact, alone. That's what this chapter is all about.

From time to time, everyone in long-term relationships hankers for the good old days when they were single and could do exactly what they wanted. You're here now, so you should be happy, yes? And yet, it seems that, as is often the case, the grass only *appears* to be greener on the other side. Remember how from where you stood before, this 'single' field over here definitely looked to have a more appealing hue to it, but for some reason, when you look back to where you were ... is it a trick of the light or does the 'attached' field you've just left, maybe have the edge? I'm labouring the point because when it comes to being happy all you can do is make the best of what you've got. It's fine to look back fondly or to the future with optimism, but you're living in the Now. Better get on with it then.

This chapter is the proverbial 'game of two halves'. It starts with all the miserable stuff you might have to deal with in the immediate future, which means you'll go in at half-time about 6–0 down. But take heart, a good team talk in the dressing room and you'll come out fighting, ready to cause one of the upsets of this year's competition. This football analogy is stretched a bit thin; better press on.

Bad stuff
Overcoming guilt

I have an ongoing argument with a friend of mine about whether my Catholic guilt is more heavily laden with sackcloth and ashes, than his Jewish guilt, which comes with its own walk-in wardrobe, packed to the ceiling with hair shirts. For both of us, even when we're living at our most squeaky clean, we can feel guilty about not feeling guilty.

After your relationship breaks up, you can feel guilty about the effect all this is having on the children, feel guilty about how your close friends and family will react, feel guilty about not having done more to save the relationship, maybe even feel guilty about leaving. Take heart, everyone goes through this, so don't let it get out of perspective. Try not to worry about it. One thing I don't think you should feel guilty about is a bit of harmless self-indulgence, in fact retail therapy can cheer you up no end.

I think the only thing you need to consider, as with all these things, is how it affects the kids. It may be that buying new clothes or going to the gym makes you feel better about yourself, so the knock-on effect is positive. You'll be happier all round, including when the children are with you and they'll pick up on that; everyone wins. As I said in Chapter 1, part of the process of becoming a great dad is to feel great about yourself as a person again. There's definitely a direct correlation between guilt and self-esteem, so the more positive you feel, the less guilt-ridden you'll be. It also helps if you have a supporter nearby (friend, family member) to tell you that you're doing fine and making a great job of bringing up the kids.

Loneliness

We all feel lonely sometimes but some of us are more prone to it than others. If you do tend to get lonely a lot of the time, you need to be aware that it can be a small step from here into depression. In the kind of macho culture where I grew up, depression was a term used for someone who seemed a bit down in the mouth; now, in more enlightened times, we can be honest enough to recognise it for the illness it is.

As with some of the stress factors I've alluded to, this is another case where a visit to the doctor is the best course of action; if it really is the case that you're just feeling a bit isolated, there are other things you can do.

Hopefully, you'll have a good support network of friends and family who will rally round and this is the time to ensure you keep in touch.

It's not a particularly blokey thing to call for a chat but I do sometimes do it. More often, I'll fire off a couple of emails to let other people know what I'm doing and catch up with their lives. Sometimes I even pretend I'm a teenager and send a text or two! All of this helps to prevent you from sinking into a maudlin state of self-pity. You learn quickly the real value of friendship but you also have to realise that it's necessary to put yourself out if you're going to get anything back. Doing a good deed for someone else, being interested in their life, listening to what their problems or triumphs are has no direct reward; at least you shouldn't expect any. However, over time 'what goes around comes around' and having an attitude which is genuinely giving almost always results in someone, somewhere, sometime repaying you for what you've done.

Anger management

When we're under stress we act out of character. We sometimes swear more, have a shorter fuse and generally lose the normal sense of proportion that our calmer self used to live by. If you have the time and energy to do so, a bit of 'situational analysis' doesn't go amiss here. If you find that you're losing your temper more often, think about who it's with and why.

I heard a really good story about a business executive who was desperately trying to control his angry outbursts, which often occurred during meetings he was running. In order to understand his feelings better, it was suggested that he marked his feelings of anger out of ten at regular intervals during the meeting (secretly, of course). After doing this on a number of occasions, he discovered that a pattern was emerging – it seemed that his ire was raised when subjects came up for discussion that he wasn't adequately prepared for or knowledge-able about. In a sense his lack of control led to frustra-tion, which quickly turned to anger. Just knowing that this was the case allowed him to manage his feelings better, by either preparing more fastidiously in advance of the meeting or recognising that he needed to exercise greater self-control when such circumstances arose.

The balance of power in each of our relationships has a great bearing on anger. We're less likely to give our boss a mouthful than someone who works for us; it's about what we believe we can get away with. In much the same way, it's easy to get angry with the kids; you're bigger than them; know more than them; have more responsibility than they do; and are the dominant party, 'in charge' of the relationship. However, that doesn't make it fair. If you get angry with them, take a minute afterwards to think about whose 'fault' it was. Did they really do something with malicious intent to make you cross or did you over-react to a situation that was part of normal life? If they wandered off in that toy shop, did they really do it to give you a rising sense of panic that they might have been abducted, or was it possibly to do with the fact that they were behaving like a child in a toy shop? There is an appropriate level of anger and they always say you should punish the action not the child, so in this case you may well show your emotions, but should be quick to explain that when they wander off you get worried you might lose them. In future if they see something that catches their eye, tell them to take you with them to look at it.

Self-esteem

I defy anyone who finds themselves single again not to suffer an occasional crisis of confidence. If you don't fit into this category, then you must be supremely arrogant.

Of course, all us big rough tough blokes are unlikely to admit to self-esteem issues too readily, we simply put on our bravest face and look the world squarely in the eye, while privately wishing it would cradle our head to its warm perfumed bosom and whisper softly 'There, there, it'll be alright'.

In the work arena, I survived many years as an executive, safe in the knowledge that I was faking it. To my amazement, my peers who were prepared to discuss the subject felt like equal phoneys, which led me to the conclusion that we all just think we're getting away with it. Even top bosses suffer this 'outsider syndrome' where they worry that someone is about to tap them on the shoulder and say 'You've been rumbled'. Now, doesn't that make you feel better about yourself? You see no one under the surface is as good as the image they portray to the world at large; we're all just doing what we can to get by.

Now you're single again, the one time when you really need to pull off this trick with consummate grace is when you have the kids. I can't imagine it helps them at all if they think their dad's a loser or if they think that their dad thinks he's a loser or if they think you think ...

Self-abuse

Being maudlin, free and alone can be a bit of a fatal combination. There's no one to check your behaviour and no one to put a brake on your excesses. These may vary for each of us but in today's society they are likely to be damaging if they get out of control. I've never yet met anyone whose over-indulgence was in good things. 'Yes, doctor, I'm a bit worried that I might be rather too fit and in shape, especially as this has come at a time when I'm doing a lot of charity work and reading all the classical works of English literature'. Much more likely is a scenario that involves substance abuse, alcohol and/or drugs, smoking, poor diet and a disregard of the protocols of when farting is allowable. Guess what, none of this makes you a better person or more attractive.

Sex, too, can become an issue, most of which I will leave to your imagination, suffice to say that the Internet can be a dangerous place for single men of a certain age. New relationships can also be a feature that complicates the landscape here (and more of how to cope with that later) but it doesn't do any harm to have a break and be on your own so that you can breathe a bit, before deciding to leap once more into the fray. When it comes to sex, it might be better to take matters into your own hands for a bit.

Good stuff

Easy then, isn't it? All we have to do is overcome guilt, loneliness, anger, low self-esteem and abuse. What on earth will we do for the rest of the day? I think one of the hardest things to come to terms with at first is that you can find yourself in emotional freefall, unable to really grab onto anything. The belief system you'd been operating within no longer applies and you have to start to rewrite your own rules.

About you

It's really not easy starting to rebuild your positive feelings if you are constantly finding ways to damage yourself. The binge indulgences I've mentioned can have the effect of dulling the senses (at least for a while) and can be an inviting place to hide. I don't want to get all transatlantic-touchy-feely here but rebuilding your self-esteem isn't about other people thinking you're a great guy; it's about whether you do. Being in control of what you put into your body is a good starting point – indulge yourself if you want to but not all the time and not to excess. It's much better used as a treat to reward yourself with than a full-time habit.

Next, it's a good idea to sort out some kind of fitness regime (if you haven't got one already) because your physical fitness has a significant effect on the state of your mental health, as mentioned in Chapter 1. Part of this is psychological in that if you look good, you can feel good too, but as we've said, exercise releases those lovely endorphins too and once they're pumping round your system, you should start to feel happier, naturally!

Practical issues

There's more to looking after yourself than a visit to the gym – you also need to get your act together on other fronts, not least the domestic one. The first step involves having a place you can call your own. Often, the former matrimonial home still houses your ex-partner and, for most of the time, the children.

Staying with friends or family is a common option for newly-estranged dads but it doesn't work in anything but the shortest of the short term. You need to find your own space, even if it's smaller than you've been used to, or rented rather than bought. The kids care less about how plush your pad is, or for that matter how flash the furniture, than they do about how you are when you see them. For a while I rented a small newish house on an estate, with a garden so small you could cut the grass with nail scissors, we had water fights in the summer and snowball fights in the winter and in between played a fair few rounds of 'Monster in the garden' (something of my own invention that involved a lot of growling and pretending to be fierce). Funnily enough, neither of the children seemed to notice that there wasn't room to swing an earthworm (though my little girl tried on a few occasions) and they still talk about that time with great affection.

I also have to say that this renting phase came about after an extended spell living with family and though I shall be eternally grateful to them for looking after me, when I look back, the first real day of 'recovery' was the day I moved into that house, *my* house. I wish I'd known how important that was – it might have prompted me into action much sooner and saved me a lot of angst.

As far as running your new home is concerned, there's a bucketful of domestic tips in Chapter 6. The most important thing of all to remember is that you need a system that suits. If you're happy living in a bit of chaos, then don't beat yourself up and spend forever dusting and hoovering. On the other hand, if you like a tidy living space, then stop yourself from stressing out by keeping it that way. Don't forget, an Englishman's home is his castle; even if it looks a bit of a tip sometimes, it is without question your castle, your tip.

You should get out more

As far as your social life goes, you now have the opportunity to make some changes here too. If you've been recently involved in a household with young children, it is very possible that you've forgotten what it's like to go out – now you can rediscover it. There's an opportunity to get back into the things you used to enjoy but haven't had time for, whether that be trainspotting or trampolining. Equally, you now have the chance to try some new stuff too (see the section on changes, p. 32 and refer back to the ten things to help your recovery in the last chapter, p. 12). You might find that friends will encourage you to indulge in lost pleasures, like night-clubs (they'll especially do this if they're still single), but choose carefully what you want to do with your social time. Seeing much younger, more beautiful people getting it on with each other, while you stand on the sidelines like some washed-up old donkey, could send you further downhill. Try to balance doing new things with some of the old familiar territory so you don't get destabilised by it all.

The day job

As I've said, work is another issue. Whether you've got it or not, whether you hate it or love it, it's a big part of what you do, what you are. Whatever your current status, try to keep work in perspective with everything else that's going on. Most of us need it to pay the bills, so disengaging with your employer (through lack of effort or application) isn't likely to help matters. On the other hand, if the stress of work, added to everything else, is really affecting your health, it's time to take stock and decide if a change of career might not suit you better. I used to believe that packing your job in was the worst possible thing anyone could do, especially if other areas of your life were in crisis. However, having witnessed at first hand the damage that a stressful job can do and the additional burden it can make you carry, I now think there is a time to call it a day and start afresh. If you can maintain the status quo at work and coast for a bit, it'll allow you some thinking time about your future career. Now is not the time to be making rash decisions, like applying for a promotion that will take you to Outer Mongolia for a few years. With so much change already happening in your life, cut your coping system some slack and allow it to deal with one thing at a time.

Routine

I've made a separate heading for routine, even though I think it's part of the practical issues. I've singled it out because I think it can sometimes be misinterpreted, after all it generally gets a bad press. As a word it conjures up rather gloomy pictures of drudgery and the everyday rut that we all sometimes feel trapped in. But it has a positive side too. Not only is it reliable (in a world that we've found to be generally less so, of late) but it provides a system that stops us having to think all the time about what happens next. In this way it saves a lot of needless energy that would otherwise have to be poured into decision-making and creates time to do the really interesting other stuff we've identified – put that way, routine doesn't seem quite such a dull fellow, after all.

We all have a tendency to be creatures of habit but you can see this as a positive if it gives you an anchor. When everything else appears to be falling apart around your ears, it's rather comforting to know that you have to get up and do certain things in a certain order each day. If you make changes to your routine, it's best if this comes as a result of a conscious decision: then you know you're doing things differently for a reason. It also re-inforces the benefits of relying on the things you know and trust. Dump your whole routine and pretty soon you won't know if you're coming or going.

Changes

And if you were starting to concern yourself with how too much routine might affect you, there's an antidote within your grasp. Take a sufficient dose of the 'changes' serum and soon your life will be perfectly back in balance. The concept of the comfort zone is a well-known one and we all feel less at ease in some situations than others. A friend of mine is a great traveller and, without meaning to, makes me feel very insular and, quite literally, unworldly. Doubtless there are things I do which he wouldn't undertake with quite such ease but equally I envy his pioneering spirit of adventure. The point of all this is that stretching yourself, breaking out of the comfort zone, is a fantastic route to fulfilment, simply because we're having a go at something we thought we could never do.

It's worth making a list of a dozen or so things you have always fancied but never had the motivation, or courage, or time, to take on, then choose one or two and give them a go – use the suggestions in the previous chapter if it helps, or come up with objectives of your own, either way it does wonders for your self-esteem.

Help me, I'm drowning!

So, there's some bad stuff to be faced, but some good stuff you can do to help you through it. Still, it will take steely reserve if you are going to achieve all this by yourself and you shouldn't see it as any kind of failing if you need help. Advice, a listening ear, a shoulder to cry on, or a mate to share it with is part of getting back to normal. Your family and oldest friends are the most reliable sources of this solace, especially when it comes to the more emotional stuff. However, new friends and contacts can be great when it comes to more practical issues; you might meet someone who can give you advice on finances, getting fit or finding places to go with the kids; don't be afraid to ask around.

Generally, when people get to hear about your change of circumstances, they will do their best to help you out but there is one final word of caution: think about who you want to know what about you. The confessional can be a dangerous place if the part of the priest is being played by your boss. A very good friend of mine, who had the dubious privilege of seeing my relationship disintegrate from the outside, said to me that each time you tell the story it will get slightly less painful, which turned out to be true. I may have told it to one or two people along the way who I now regret burdening with it. Thinking back, I also feel rather foolish for having shared so much with people whose normal level of intimacy with me didn't stretch beyond sharing the odd beer together. (With luck they went on to drink so much after I left that they didn't remember the next day.)

Being single

Overall, being single isn't a bad place to be, unless you desperately yearn for the love of a good woman, in which case read on as there's a whole section on this later. For the time being though, you can start to see how the different bits of your life can be sorted out and how you can feel good about yourself once again. As far as the kids are concerned, the most important spin-off from this is that you'll be happy and in most cases, when you are, so are they. Suddenly, you're a great dad.

Ten great things about being single again

In case this chapter has depressed you a bit, I've put together my own list of things to cheer you up. I bet you can come up with a few of your own, if you stop and think about it.

1. *You have the power of the remote control, you never have to watch any girly stuff on telly again and instead, if you want, can select from things like Men and Motors, the footie, repeats of Dad's Army or pro-celebrity nude drag racing on the Testosterone-Plus channel.*

2. *The toothpaste tube will always be squeezed your way (mostly in an orderly fashion from the bottom up, in my experience).*

3. *While we're in the bathroom, you can forget about the issue of the toilet seat. Just like the Grand Old Duke of York's men you can be satisfied that when it was up it was up and when it was down it was down and when it was only half way up you risked catching your tackle in it.*

4. *You can sleep diagonally in a double bed, meaning that neither your feet nor your head need ever be cold again.*

5. *A night with the lads will never be an issue.*
   I could never understand why women in general seem to think that dark satanic rituals involving buxom virgins take place on such nights. Men go out, talk about football, talk about women (in an obtuse and non-threatening way), talk about politics and, frankly, most of the time talk bollocks, then they go home again. I find it hard to think of a more innocent pleasure.

6. *DIY can be left undone – forever, if necessary.*

7. *You never have to feign a headache or be on the receiving end of one.*

8. *You make the rules; for yourself, for your children, for how you choose to live your life (be a bit careful with this one).*

9. *Your phone bill will be drastically reduced (unless you've got teenagers and they should be using their mobiles, anyway). This is because we never call our mothers as often as we should and it has been scientifically proven that no bloke-to-bloke phone call has ever lasted longer than one minute*

*forty-two seconds (and that includes the time
taken to discuss all necessary pleasantries).*

10. *The world is your oyster. Try to pick one that's
got a pearl in it, otherwise wash down with 11
others and several pints of Guinness.*

3

Walk a mile in their shoes

With all the stuff that kids have to cope with once their parents are flying solo, the last thing they need is for *you* to start playing up, that's their job, even their right, so take some time to think about how it is for them and make some conscious decisions about how *you'll* behave in future. Here are five 'behaviours' that I set for myself once I'd realised that drifting along wasn't doing me or the children any good.

Show love and affection

How open and giving we are with our love is dependent on many factors. I know blokes who will happily hug and kiss their kids in public at the drop of a hat; alternatively, I've got friends who are much more stand-offish and would consider any physical contact as well out of bounds.

A good personal benchmark is to consider how you treated the kids in this regard before you were estranged in the first place and make an effort, especially in the early days of separation, to magnify your demonstrative affection, to go a bit beyond where you might have done previously. Love and affection (no matter how you choose to show it) is like an endless supply of magic sticking plaster that covers emotional wounds and at least gives them a chance to eventually heal themselves. You can't take away all the hurt but you can give succour to troubled souls and let them see that no matter what has happened, there is still something they can count on.

Our ability to give love and our need to receive it is something constant throughout our lives and fortunately it's neither metered nor costly. However, when we are grown we also have the ability to rationalise this part of our existence in the context of everything else that's happening to us. Children are less able to do so – the world is much more black and white for them. The younger they are, the more we need to exaggerate and emphasise our behaviours; when you 'baby talk' with a newborn you tend to make huge gestures of pleasure, beaming like an idiot and speaking in a wildly exaggerated voice ('Who's a lovely boy then?!'). This diminishes to the point where a low grunt or simple curl of the lip is sufficient to greet a teenager; in fact, anything else would be regarded as hugely embarrassing. For the time being, you're trying to do something in between.

Don't burden them

You might find your own coping mechanism a bit stretched during the stressful business of finding your single feet again, but this really isn't the time to use the children as stress counsellors, they have their own stuff to cope with. We've all been in a position where we've had a 'my life's shittier than your life' competition, which involves acting like a dog in a manger on the sort of day when no one wants to buy your master's *Big Issue*. You may think that the challenges they face are less numerous or onerous than yours – all they have to think about is whose house they're at. You've got the mountain of other problems, including emotional stress, money worries, keeping a roof over their heads, getting divorced, working too many hours ... the list goes on. But just because you can make a longer list doesn't mean that their issues are less *complex* than yours.

I think the only time they need to know what your suffering is, is when you've taken your stress out on them needlessly, so if you lose it with them and are big enough to admit to yourself that it was more to do with your inability to keep all the plates spinning than anything inherently malicious in their behaviour, I think it's OK to explain that you're shorter tempered than usual because you've got things on your mind. Getting out the credit card statement and pointing to the outstanding balance may help to substantiate your case but it doesn't add much to the understanding of the kids, so it's better to keep the angst a general thing. If you do face these circumstances, there's every chance that the kids (sensitive as they are) will pick up on this and start to worry on your behalf, so I'm always at pains to point out that all problems are transient and the current difficulties will soon blow over, so it's nothing for them to be concerned about.

Be grown up

If the wheels have fallen off your world, you can bet that the same fate has befallen the children but you're the adult here and they can rightly expect that you'll take charge of things. After all, they've been used to looking to you to 'sort any situation' in the past; you've fed them and bathed them, said 'there, there' when they'd been hurt and tied countless shoelaces, so from where they're standing, you're the reliable source of all knowledge, comfort and solace. If they're now in a position where their world has been destabilised, who else do you expect them to turn to but you?

If at all possible try to hold yourself together during the times they are with you, even if before and after you're not fit to be allowed out. The tremendous resilience of children means that they can probably be relied on to support you if the need arises, but it's no fun looking back and realising that they were *your* emotional crutch, when it should have been the other way round.

I'm not advocating that amongst all this you avoid any discussion of what is going on but it's much better if they set the agenda, rather than you imposing a home version of 'Question Time' upon them. Try to be matter of fact about the issues, without coming across as unfeeling. It's easy to talk endlessly about the past and how we all wish things had turned out differently but it's the here and now which is important, along with what you expect to happen next. In this regard it's easy to make all kinds of promises that you'll forget (at this stage of break-up it's sometimes hard to even remember your own name) but you can bet your life that if you say 'It'll all be fine and we can go to the funfair together in the summer', they'll remember even if you don't and there's nothing worse than a broken promise to a child.

Overall, you need to appear to be in control (at a time when you're probably not), so you'll be testing your acting skills to the full. It will help if you think about the things that are already sorted out and put the most emphasis on them, but if you're still unsure where you're going to live or how you are going to afford it (because you haven't yet settled the financial side with your ex-partner), try to avoid too much in-depth discussion on these topics. The chances are that some of these more practical issues won't have even struck the children as important; they'll just assume everything will get sorted. My advice would be to leave them in this happy state of ignorance and devote your energies to overcoming some of the practical difficulties at a time when they're with their mum.

Be balanced

There's a great temptation as a 'weekend dad' to try to make your time with the children perfect in every way. From your own point of view the joy of seeing them can make you try to create a kind of romantic Utopia where everyone is happy and voices are never raised in anger. Looking at it through their eyes, especially in the early days, a visit to you will seem like an event. That's fine for a while but the state you are really trying to achieve is that being with you is just a part of normal life, the venue and personnel may have changed, but it's nothing particularly out of the ordinary.

It may seem that I'm saying you need to have a 'no treats' policy, which under the circumstances would look a bit harsh, but in reality the emphasis here is on balance, that's to say you should think about how much you would have treated them in the past and try not to let the current situation force you into doing things too differently. I come back here to one of the main themes of this book, that being a great dad is more about the experiences you give them than the things you buy them. Whatever stuff they acquire is transient but their memories, if they're good ones, will last forever.

We've all heard, countless times, that life is full of ups and downs and I think that's a good thing. If my children are 'down' for any reason, I talk to them about the contrasts that are necessary for us to appreciate the good things in life, so I say that you have to sometimes have bad times so that you can properly appreciate the good times – if there were no contrast there would be no basis for comparison. As a grown-up, do you really 'wish it could be Christmas every day'? I doubt it, because we can rationalise the fact that special times are only special because they're not happening all the time.

In much the same way, if you lose the natural balance of treating the children, it will soon become the norm and once that happens it's hard to make anything seem special. The further downside of this is that when you spoil them they not surprisingly act exactly like 'spoiled children', as their expectation rises (and your ability to deliver against it falls), so their gratitude will diminish and you're on a downward spiral of having to provide more and more treats just to maintain the same level of appreciation.

Children have an innate ability to surprise us again and again, and often it's the small things, inconsequential in our eyes, that really strike a chord with them. If you can develop the ability to see the world through their eyes, you'll come to realise that their favourite meal or a later bedtime can be just as much of a treat as a visit to the cinema or park.

Once again, balance is the key, so if you do allow them an extra half-hour at the end of the day to watch 'World's Craziest Police Camcorder Chases', make sure they know that it's been your decision to give them the leeway, not just the fact that you couldn't be bothered to chase them to bed.

Be happy

Yes, I know you may never have felt more miserable but does everyone need to know that? One of my most treasured possessions is a laminated bookmark made for me by my daughter when she was seven. Her teacher helped the class make the bookmarks as Father's Day presents, with the instruction they should contain a drawing of dad (always a cause of great hilarity) and some suitable words to accompany it. Bless her heart, she drew me with more hair than I've really got (or ever had) and wrote 'I love my daddy because he is always happy'. Of course, this simply isn't true, but during the times when I'm not, if I read the words, it's hard not to smile and I can't think of any better way to be perceived by your offspring.

If we accept the theory that from the time they are born babies emulate our behaviours, copy the things we do and mimic our actions, then if we have a sunny demeanour, it's much more likely that they will too. Equally, you know that if you're distracted or down, the children are quick to pick up on your mood and it's not long before they are feeling the same emotions themselves.

I'm not a psychologist so there's no real science here but I do have a firm belief that mood is a state of mind and if we *act* in a certain way, we *become* a certain way. What I'm saying is that if you look to the outside world like you have a devil-may-care attitude, then before long you start to feel that way too. OK, I've heard the lyrics of Smokey Robinson's 'Tears of a clown' and like everyone else I've had times when the last thing I felt like doing was being sociable and cheery but in the main if you put on a happy face, your mood will follow along behind; quite happily in fact.

In a way that is the whole point of this book, because your happiness is not only important to you as an individual human being, it's also a critical element of how good your kids feel. I suppose the great trick is harmonising your happiness, that's to say making sure that what you do and how you behave isn't at odds with what makes them happy. I've devoted the whole of Chapter 19 to this subject as a springboard to your future, but for the time being I think it's worth my recounting a bit of personal experience, along with a story that is inherently funny, made my kids laugh and helped teach me that you have to be able to see the funny side of life.

The relevance of all this in my quest to be a great single dad is that sometimes life is cruel and no matter how hard you try, your children are going to learn this lesson for themselves; they're going to discover things like disappointment and feelings of being let down. But finding the funny side is a great antidote and helps to build up the kind of resilience we all need to be able to cope with the modern world. As an illustration, I'll share with you one of my most embarrassing moments and defy you to not find it funny.

While I was still married (and before the children had arrived), I went skiing in France with my wife and another couple, the deal being that we took it in turns to cook the evening meal. Now my inability to master the French language is matched only by my lack of understanding of the metric system, having been brought up in the era of 'old money' where good old pounds and ounces were the currency of the butcher's shop.

Spaghetti Bolognese seemed like the kind of fare you'd need after a day on the piste, not least because it would help soak up the vast quantities of cheap red wine that we were bound to drink, so we entered a packed charcuterie (packed with indigenous residents, I should point out), me armed to the teeth with what I believed to be the correct French phrases. Eventually my turn arrived and I asked the genial French butcher for what I thought to be the correct quantity (in grammes) of *boeuf hâché* (that's mince!) required for a hearty feast for four hungry Brits.

The French have a kind of style when they're serving you that we can never hope to emulate, so the gentleman in question drew a sheet of waxed paper from a pile and turned round to the electric mincing machine set on the back counter. Sticking out of the hopper at the top was the biggest piece of beef I have ever seen and he carefully held the paper beneath the apparatus. It had two buttons on the front, green for start and red for stop (it seems that this is a universal language). First, he pressed the green button and then a millisecond later, with a flourish, hit the red one. To the great amusement of the rest of the shop, he turned back to me and outstretched his arm over the counter to show me the fruits of his labours, a walnut-sized blob of minced beef, with the single immortal entreaty, 'Monsieur?'

What was hilarious about the whole incident, is that he never once cracked a smile or raised an eyebrow, as if people entered his shop all the time and asked for a quantity of meat that would feed a carnivorous mouse. And some say the Continentals have no sense of humour.

The other fascinating thing is that your kids always seem to find these stories hysterical too, they enjoy it all the more when you make a fool of yourself, perhaps because for most of the time they see you as a figure of respectability, capability and responsibility. It's that contrast thing again. Be happy, life's too short not to.

The funny thing about happiness is that it is infectious, so the more of it you have, the greater the likelihood of the children catching it. Making children laugh out loud is also extremely easy and they especially love it when things go wrong, which is something you can engineer if you feel like playing to the crowd. Falling in the pool 'accidentally on purpose' is an obvious one but you can also amuse them by inadvertently pouring the whole bottle of bubble bath into the tub, which will result in a mountain of foam and cost you in the region of ninety pence (a really good investment in my opinion). The other shock tactic I like to use now and then is to pretend to be angry and shout at the children, something like 'Do you know what's wrong with you two today?' and when they go quiet and unsure, follow it up with 'You haven't had enough chocolate!' It gets them every time!

So, there are my five aspirational behaviours, drawn together with the benefit of some experience and a pinch or two of hindsight, in the knowledge that the way you behave has a dramatic effect on how well the children are able to cope with a break-up. I think we owe it to them to do the best we can for their sakes, as they'll have difficulty coming to terms with why it's all happened. People say that children always blame themselves for the split between their parents and I'm not sure you can avoid that. However, it does no harm to tell them that it's *not* their fault and that despite the fact that you can't all get on as a family unit any more that doesn't mean they're loved any less, by either of you.

With young children they find it hard to articulate their emotions. It might be that they simply don't yet have the language or logic skills to work out why they feel the way they do, so what can often result is a change in their behaviour; it's as if they're showing you how they feel without being able to say it. This is all rather unpredictable because they can either go quiet and become introverted, or can start to play up at every possible opportunity; whatever happens it's not their fault. Their emotions may include confusion, regret, insecurity or anger, which are tough enough to deal with when you're a grown-up, even harder as a toddler. It's over five years since my own marriage break-up and it is my confirmed belief that as an adult you go through two years of madness before you start to emerge on the other side. Such was my confusion and desire just to get through each day, I actually don't remember very accurately what it was like, other than the fact it was pretty awful. I can recall even less about how the children reacted, such was my rather shallow self-obsession at the time.

Because of this I decided it would be a good idea to let them have a voice here, so I asked them 'How was it for you?' I was surprised, shocked and humbled at their reaction because asking them to recall what it felt like reduced both of them, spontaneously, to tears within seconds; each recounted some particular aspect that has stayed with them and I felt stupid for having asked the question. What did I expect? That they'd both say 'Actually dad, we didn't think it made much difference when you left'? Knowing how much upset I'd caused them hardly made me feel better about myself, but all I can say to counterbalance this is that after a few minutes they calmed down and assured me that despite the trauma at the time, they now didn't give our circum-stances a second thought, it's just the way life is. I made a huge mistake here in assuming things on behalf of both the children, which made me think about how easy it is to just see them as your kids rather than as distinctly different human beings (albeit who look a bit like you) with their own feelings, opinions and emotions. It was a timely reminder to let them have their say more often, but more than that, to really listen to what they think and take account of it, no matter how 'inconvenient' it may be when it doesn't fit in with what I want.

Concentrating on how you behave under these circum-stances can go some way towards easing the pain but there are other practical things you can do to lessen the blow. Becoming a bit nomadic and drifting from one parent's home to the other never seems to faze them but the important point about this is that you do make a conscious effort to create a home at your place. If at all possible, make sure they have their own room, their own space, which you can fill with familiar things so it's not a new experience every time they visit. They need an anchor to maintain stability and this is a great starting point.

Try to do as much preparation before each visit to minimise the hassle they'll suffer, so make sure you've got food in (this gets easier over time) and enough clothes of an appropriate type, so they don't have to look like a tramp when they're out with you. Accept too the fact that you will need to put yourself out more – if a favourite teddy gets left at mum's and they simply can't sleep without it, you'll be a better dad if you go back for it rather than say 'That's just tough, this is the way life is from now on'.

It also helps if you've done some pre-planning on what to do with them. It doesn't have to be wall-to-wall entertainment but having a few options up your sleeve is much better than just busking it and then wondering why they're bored or grumpy, but more of this later.

Finally, a word about the contact you have with the children when they're not with you. I think the more regular this is, the better – even if it's only a few minutes on the phone each night you get the chance to catch up with their day and you miss less of what goes on in their lives. You have to be conscious of the fact that when you call it's their agenda though and not expect them to drop everything to be attentive to you. I can tell you now that given the choice between me and Bart Simpson, the kids would rather listen to that yellow fella any day. My advice, under these circumstances, is to check the TV schedule, and try to call at a time their favourite cartoon isn't on.

There's a ton of stuff to cope with at the time of the relationship breakdown and looking back I don't think I did it particularly well. My greatest regret is not taking enough time and making sufficient effort to see the world from where the children were looking at it. I really wish I'd made the effort to 'walk a mile in their shoes'. I don't think for a minute that, if I had, everything would have been fine and dandy, it's always going to hurt them, but it's not their fault and every ounce of effort you make to help them see that takes you that bit closer to being a great single dad.

4

Single mums

Logic dictates that for every single dad there must be a single mum, so this is a chapter about what I think it's like for them. If you're still feeling a great deal of animosity towards the mother of your children, then you might not see the relevance of this, but the important part to remember is the role she plays in the life of your kids on an ongoing basis. The sooner you come to terms with this, the better, because understanding what life is like for the children when they're *not* with you is part of being a great dad.

Because you are now sharing the responsibility for child care, whatever one of you does will affect the other. This is not just in terms of the regime that's in place at either household, it's also about more fundamental issues over how much time each of you gets with the children. If you have contact at weekends and aren't the full-time carer, this could all change if you end up in a situation where your former wife can't cope. It doesn't matter whether she acknowledges your contribution or not, without her life would be very different.

on the other side of the fence

I may be generalising here but my guess is that life is pretty tough for most single mums. Without the two of you together it's doubtful she'll have as much disposable income, after all two can only live as cheaply as one if you remain in the same household!

Added to that is the responsibility that goes with child care. This is difficult enough as a couple but when you have to take all the day-to-day decisions with no back-up, that's quite a weight to carry. I noticed, once we'd split up, how hard it is to be on your own, especially if the children are being difficult. Before, there was someone who could step in and take the heat out of the situation or, where appropriate, back you up. Suddenly, that's gone and you're faced with having no arbitrator, no sense check. I can only imagine that's even harder when you have the kids for most of the time.

I'm not going to step into the dangerous territory of stereotyping and suggest that women only do the lovely fluffy things like arranging a vase of flowers, or that men are physiologically better suited to car maintenance, it's just that the sheer volume of stuff that needs to be done in a house with kids makes it much easier if there are two of you sharing the load. For this reason, having a man around the house is probably quite useful at times, if a little irritating. Maybe it's only after we've gone that they realise we did have some function to perform.

Tied up with all this is the fact that we can't really 'role model' the opposite sex for our children. Boys in partic-ular have a problem here. Progressively, they are falling behind their female counterparts in terms of their education and there are some schools of thought that subscribe to the view that fathers should try harder to show by example not only the benefit of learning but the way to do it. This is just one example but there are countless more scenarios when children would benefit from having the continual presence of both parents to learn their behaviours from.

Money

No wonder it's often branded the root of all evil – when couples reach the last resort of the courtroom, it's often the issue of money that's highest on the agenda. There was once a time when the legal system found very much in favour of the woman but I'm given to understand, by an acquaintance who is a Relate counsellor, that this position has changed somewhat over recent years.

In fairness, the legal system surrounding divorce aims to put the interests of the children at the forefront. You can argue forever about who is getting which CDs but the important thing you'll miss is that though the two of you can no longer get along, it's the innocent 'victims', the kids, who are at greatest risk of suffering. On this basis it's of no real benefit to them to see mum living in a four-bedroom detached house and when they go to dad's, they all have to squash into his one-bedroom squalid bedsit. For this reason there tends to be a more even split of the spoils than before but you still have to take account of other important factors, like the normal scenario of dads being able to earn more (because sex discrimination does happen and it's harder to get a top job when you're balancing full-time child care), added to the fact that in many cases the children will spend more time in maternal surroundings.

When I look back at my own settlement, it's not the money that really matters. I think what's really interesting is my attitude, irrespective of what the final figures looked like. Right at the start I was anxious that the disruption to the children was minimised, so I tried for a time to keep the former matrimonial home on the go, which left me living with my brother or sister for most of the time. When I realised that this couldn't go on and we'd have to sell up, we spent a lot of money on solicitors who wrote snotty letters to each other on our joint behalf (bad mistake). However, when it was all done and dusted some people thought I'd got a rather raw deal. I never looked at it like that because I knew that wherever my wife ended up would be where my kids lived for most of the time, so why try to do a 50:50 deal when they weren't with me for half the time?

Whatever the circumstances of your personal deal, it would be unusual for your ex-partner to be as financially well off as before, so being a single mum carries with it a stiff financial penalty.

When couples do split up each party slinks away to lick their wounds, often with a camp of supporters who will tell them that they're better off without the other half. Tied in with this they encourage each of you to screw the other; clearly sensible advice because I bet the children never notice when you are involved in all-out war over money. Yeah, right.

Stigma

I always think it's funny the images that are conjured up by certain words or phrases: why do 'freshly cut' sandwiches always sound better than just plain 'sandwiches'? Across the board we form pictures in our heads, based on our experiences, our cultures and the prejudices we learn from the media. Close your eyes and think of the phrase 'single mother' and you might see a plucky, hard-working saint, juggling work and child care, while whipping up a tasty quiche with her spare hand, or you might see a sixteen-year-old pregnant girl with a toddler in a buggy, cheeseburger in one hand and fag in the other. Somehow there's nothing very wholesome about the phrase 'single mother'.

On the other hand, 'single dad' can sound quite cool, a bit put upon, doing his best to provide a role model for his children, while in touch with his feminine sensitive side, whipping up a tasty quiche with his spare hand.

It's not fair but it's there and it's part of the plethora of troubles that single mothers have to deal with. I bet it looks even more unfair from where they're standing and probably does very little to build their self-esteem at a time when they could usefully employ some.

New men

Whether you wanted to part or not, the reality of the situation is that beside the kids you are now both completely free emotional agents. For many blokes this is fine because they have time on their hands and the opportunity to seek out a new partner if they so wish.

Again, this must be an area of greater difficulty for your former partner. Not only has she less freedom, because she's looking after your kids, but the fact is they are the very thing which is likely to put potential suitors off most quickly. Lots of guys don't want the responsibility of other people's children and even if they do, there's nothing to say that they will all get on or that there won't be a deliberate attempt at sabotage from children who see the new interloper as yet another obstacle between the two of you reconciling your differences.

Nevertheless, ex-wives do meet new men and if this happens, it is pointless getting jealous or difficult about it, even if you are naturally so inclined: *you have no right of ownership here*. Instead try to take the view of the courts that it's the children's happiness which is paramount and if at all possible seek the objective view of a trusted friend. The best possible situation is if the children see that their mum has met someone who makes her happy and they all get along well. If at some point he moves in, you have to accept the fact that he will perform some of the duties that you used to, but equally you need to be self-confident enough in your own abilities and relationship with the children that you are and will always continue to be their dad. It may seem like I'm trying to stretch your compassion too far here but I think it's worth being more accommodating during this new courtship to give them a chance to see if they get on. Being deliberately rude or not accounting for the fact that they may want to be together on their own (meaning you need to be flexible on child care) is likely to help scupper the whole thing before it's got off the ground and I'm not sure who the winner is there.

Togetherness

You may now find that you're living in separate houses but there are times when you still need to present a united front to the children. On a day-to-day basis it benefits nobody if you are continually at daggers drawn, it makes the kids jumpy because they have to be careful not to say the wrong thing about the other parent to the other party, 'Oh, you should have seen Dad on Saturday, he was really drunk!' Beyond this the values set that you bring them up by needs to be an area of common ground. If one of you lets them swear and stay up late and the other imposes strict discipline, they have to spend their lives adapting to your individual personal styles. Of course, there will be grey areas where one gives them more leeway than the other, but at the core there needs to be consistency.

In my case, I think we're lucky that our relationship is civil in the extreme without being likely to lead to reconciliation, so we even go so far as to celebrate family occasions, like birthdays, by spending some time as a 'family'. If it's a party for one of the children, we both attend, join in and share the cost; if it's either of ours, we get together for a ceremonial blowing out of candles and chorus of 'Happy Birthday', which the children enjoy immensely, mainly because they get to eat cake.

Similarly, on parents' evenings at school we attend together, though this wasn't always the case, partly because of logistics – I couldn't always be there at the same time – and also because, especially in the early days, I felt that my role in their education would be somewhat different due to the fact that they weren't with me as much. Now it seems more sensible to make it a joint experience, then whatever the outcome, you can share in the pride and triumph or have a grown-up discussion about any 'problem' areas that your children might need help with.

The future

If you think all this is too touchy-feely and can never see a time when you'll be able to exchange a civil word, then take a minute to think about the future. At some point it's likely that your children will want to get married themselves. I guess it's strange enough going to such an event, knowing you'll bump into all those ex-in-laws you haven't seen for years, but why spoil the day by giving your kids the impossible task of worrying about who to invite on either side of the family?

For both of you staying civil shouldn't be nearly as hard as staying married. Apart from anything else you have a strictly limited amount of time together now, so you should be able to get through it without arguing. While we're on the subject, the way you communicate now is important so by all means use email or text or a note with the kids when appropriate, but when it comes to the really important things that affect their future, be grown up enough to sit down and discuss it face to face, like grown-ups, really.

If you're still struggling, then contemplate for a moment the divorced dad of my acquaintance who spoke not a word to his ex-wife from the minute they split up. When I asked him how he kept in touch with the children, he said that he'd bought them both mobile phones so he could call them direct. I'm sure he thought he'd beaten the system, but it hardly provides an ideal role model on relationships for the kids.

Lots of couples who were once so much in love seem to end up hating each other but when their former blissful state resulted in the creation of new human beings, a lifelong responsibility came along with it. Only in extreme circumstances will the children stop loving one parent and in the long run it will probably be to their detriment, so we have to find ways of making room for our ex-partners, at least in our children's lives, if not our own.

The state of 'hate' is for most people fairly transient, though some do manage, through a great effort, to sustain it forever. It's mostly brought about by the trauma of break-up but time heals these wounds and it's really in the best interests of the children if you can be polite to one another and explain to your offspring that just because your own marriage/relationship didn't work out, it doesn't mean that they're a bad thing. I don't want my children to grow up being so cynical about the state of matrimony that they shy away from it altogether and I do want them to know that even if, with the best will in the world, things don't work out, there is life afterwards.

5

When I was a lad ...

Things just aren't the same any more, are they? I mean, especially 'the youth of today', they're not like we were. This is a chapter about how and why things have changed both for good and bad, and why it's important to recognise the difference between then and now when it comes to bringing up our own children.

My firmly held belief is that child rearing needs context if it's to be successful.

> **If you try to bring your kids up by using the template of your youth, you're in for trouble because things have moved on.**

We need, for their sake, to embrace this Brave New World but first, for our own comfort, let's start with a warm cuddly reminisce about 'the way we were'. I'm lucky in being able to look back to my own childhood with a real sense of affection. I felt safe, secure, loved, and remember mostly happy times – ain't nostalgia great?

Recently, I discovered in a magazine a photograph of a busy street corner in Liverpool in December 1957, the month of my birth. This was made all the more relevant by the fact that I was born and for the most part brought up on Merseyside, so it was a good snapshot of what life was like for my folks around that time. The cars looked very old-fashioned, the people dressed in 'sensible' clothes (most of the men wore hats; I wish we still did, a hat is a marvellous way of expressing yourself), the shops on the high street all carried the name of some independent proprietor, rather than the chain stores that dominate our urban landscape today and, of course, the whole picture was in black and white. Maybe, when I think about it, life was after all a bit monochrome back then.

You see, that's the downside of nostalgia, we tend only to remember what we want to rather than what it was really like. I'll return to this later but for now let's look at the significant changes that have occurred since I was a lad, since, in the view of my children, the Dark Ages.

Technology

This is first on the list because it's not only the biggest change but as far as I can see it will continue to be so in the foreseeable future. I'm sure if you stepped back a further generation, our parents would think that they'd seen some changes, the introduction of the family motor car (mass-produced for the first time so that more and more people could afford them) and marvellous labour-saving devices like automatic washing machines, fridges, cookers, etc., not to mention a whole new world in home entertainment in the form of the radiogram and television.

But all this is nought compared to what *we've* seen in the last 30 years or so. Electronics, computing and the microchip have revolutionised the way we live our lives; even if you wanted to remain a low-tech Luddite, you couldn't avoid technology touching you at every turn, from the cash point machine to the humble Dolby Surround Sound Home Cinema system. The impact of this has had significant repercussions for many of the other items on this list, so read on.

communication

A pet subject for me, this one, in fact I even wrote a book on it once. Bad communication is blamed for all the ills of business and beyond. When marriages break down, it's often cited as a primary cause. As Cliff once sang, 'It's so funny, how we don't talk any more'. The really big changes, though, have occurred because of the number of channels of communication that have opened up. Now we need never be out of touch with one another through email and the like, and with the rest of the world via satellite TV or online news gathering. What is often forgotten in the midst of all this high-tech gadgetry is that communication is about more than the *ability* to send and receive messages, it's about the *desire*. You can be connected to the world in a million-

and-one ways but if no one wants to get in touch, you can be the loneliest guy on the planet.

work

Hard labour has been replaced for many of us by what the experts call a 'knowledge society', so it's no longer what we can do physically that's important but what we know, how we think and our application of that 'intelligence'. Manufacturing in the UK has been on the wane for years and increasingly that's been replaced by service-driven industry. Our sons and daughters are going to face very different choices when the time comes to enter the world of work. What's quite funny about all this is that the experts of long ago made predictions about how work would change and got it completely wrong. They thought that all this change would mean we'd be liberated to live a life of increasing leisure; instead we've ended up putting in more hours than ever, resulting in us becoming 'cash rich' but 'time poor'. If you're really concerned about the whole work/life balance thing, you need to keep this equation in mind because it's unlikely that you'll become rich in both ways. If what you earn is the thing that really drives your happiness, then fine, but if you hanker to spend more time doing the things you want – like taking your kids to the park, for example – then the greatest likelihood is that you'll have to forego some of the dosh. Oh, how we tittered at the wackiness of 'The Good Life' where Tom and Barbara gave up the rat race to live a more pastoral existence, underpinned by their ability to survive off the land and their wits. When you look at the stresses and strains that most of us suffer at work, consider the fallout on family life and our health, it somehow doesn't seem quite so ludicrous any more, does it?

Wealth

Before I get too po-faced, it's worth remembering that we're all better off in pure cash terms than ever before. 'We've never had it so good'. In itself this is no bad thing as it gives us opportunities that were never afforded previous generations. Spending money on stuff can be a good thing, a new car provides us with a safer, faster and more comfortable way of getting from A to B; with satellite navigation systems installed we won't get lost on the way, and built-in screens for the back-seat passengers to watch their favourite DVDs pretty much ensure that the old cry of 'Are we there yet?' (just as you reach the bottom of your road) is consigned to the past. In the same way, the introduction of the MP3 player means that you can relax to your favourite tunes whenever you like. Just think how this enhances your life – if you're on the tube you no longer have to sit and stare at the underground map opposite, or worry about catching the eye of the big bloke with the shaven head, you can just lose yourself in Mantovani (sorry, bad choice). Personally, I favour less material and more experiential uses of money, it's not so much what you can *buy* with it but what you can *do*. You can travel the world and literally broaden your horizons, go and enjoy a really fantastic meal, take singing lessons, learn how to fly (in a plane, obviously). In this day and age if you haven't got a list of 50 things to do before you die, you need your head testing and if you're going to achieve them, then money is a great asset.

Family

I'm using the term in its broadest possible sense here, so yes, our family life has changed, but sometimes I think it's the extended outer edges of it that have altered the most. All those aunties and uncles we used to have, who were really just friends of your mum and dad, don't seem to exist any more. Next door to us, when I was born, we had Uncle Bert and Auntie Edie. I spent hours in their house and she entertained me endlessly without a Gameboy in sight. I can remember the thrill of helping her make a cup of tea and the ultimate treat was being allowed to have one of Uncle Bert's Zubes (the kind of cough sweet you needed when you smoked 60 Capstan Full Strength a day; that's Bert, of course, not me) from a tin on the bedside table.

Siblings too, both older and younger, had a greater influence over us, especially in large families. Many older children had learned parenting skills way before they left home as they'd been called upon to look after the 'young 'uns' from an early age. Contraception has cut the number of large families; child care (professional and paid for) removed the need for sibling rearing. For us as parents, many of the changes to family life have made things easier but there is a downside too. Not having anyone close by to baby-sit or call upon for advice has left us isolated in our parental duties and in the early days especially it's great to be able to call upon someone who's 'been there' for advice. I recall changing my first nappy and worrying that I'd put it on too tightly. In the end I asked the advice of the visiting gritty northern midwife. 'Is he skriking?', she asked me (I took this to mean crying, forgive me if I've got it wrong). 'No', I replied flatly. 'Well then', she said 'it's not too tight, is it?' Bloody obvious, really, but it would have been good not to have learned it from a stranger.

Society

The way we *live*, the way we *think*, the way we *are* are all different to how it used to be and inevitably that collective change in our psyche means our world is now a very different place, particularly when it comes to the way we interact with each other. Along with the passing of all those non-blood-related relatives we seem to have become more insular than ever. The latchkey society, when you just popped into other people's houses, and they into yours, is now consigned to an age gone by. In fact, with the alarming increase of gated communities you now not only need your own key but a six-digit PIN to get past the front portal, with its steel re-inforced spikes, barbed-wire fencing and strategically placed snipers and land mines. You get the feeling, don't you, that we're not as welcoming as we once were. There are lots of the factors that we've already considered above which have contributed to this, we work longer hours, are more disposed to entertain ourselves at home with the plethora of technology that is available and don't interact in a community-based way that was founded on being part of a long-established family in the area. It's ironic too that the communication channels which allow us so many more ways of 'talking' to each other make us more disposed to sit at home and join in 'global communities' on the Internet rather than pop next door for a cup of tea and a gossip.

I think too that the media has had a large part to play in shaping our view of the world and there are many things which we now perceive to be fact, simply because it is in the interests of mass communicators to exaggerate certain aspects of the way we live for reasons of sensationalism. They're not solely to blame though; if we didn't consume what they fed us so voraciously, they wouldn't stoop to write about it in the first place. The media adage is 'if it bleeds, it leads' so a story of murder is always more likely to hit the headlines than the sad tale of the cat stuck up the tree.

Obsession with celebrity is equally a winner. Former editor of *The Sun* Kelvin McKenzie was interviewed after the death of Diana and asked if it was really necessary to intrude into her personal life in such a way. He replied by saying that whenever they put her photograph on the front page of *The Sun*, they sold more copies than the days they didn't, so who is the more guilty, them or us?

Danger

A fallout from the way the media reports is that we seem to feel in more danger now than when we were growing up. This is an especially important element of how we treat our own children. We drive them to school and pick them up, we don't let them go and play in the park with other kids (unless they've got their mobile and can text us at any time) and we discourage them from any interaction with people who we have not carefully selected and had police-checked.

But are things really more dangerous? Are there more muggings, murders, sex abuse crimes? I was always brought up being told that I 'shouldn't talk to strangers'. I was a mere eight-year-old when Myra Hindley and Ian Brady were jailed for life, so was it actually an age of innocence? I'm as shocked and saddened as anyone when I hear about a 'James Bulger' or a 'Soham murder' case but whether these things are on the increase or not isn't the issue for me as a parent. The real issue is that the media makes me *believe* that I have to protect my children more.

Expectation

If you distil all the factors I've talked about, the result is that our expectations as citizens have changed. We want more and we get more, we're more cautious, wary, scared. We're probably more selfish and less willing to help others and we're so concerned for our children that we have a greater tendency than ever to wrap them in cotton wool and keep them from the nasty things in life.

But if *our* expectations have changed, it's nothing compared to our offsprings. They are subjected to images of success, beauty, wealth and happiness that have been manufactured merely to sell 'product', which increases their aspiration all the time and when you add to this the peer pressure they experience from their friends, with their designer clothes and the latest gadgets, it's easy to see how we can get caught in a trap of never-ending expenditure.

So many things have changed and it's little wonder that we get nostalgic sometimes. The inevitability of life is that the older we get, the more fondly we look back. This is all well and good but you have to remember the *real* value of the past and why it is important for your children. We learn from history and heritage, learn what makes us who we are and how we behave and gain an insight into the right way to do things. At the most basic level, heredity gives us clues about our future – for example, when it comes to health issues. A family with a history of heart disease gives a pointer to today's generation that they'll have to try extra hard to look after themselves as their risk factor is greater than average. Less obvious attributes than our physiology are also important. Character traits like musical ability or an adventurous spirit can equally have an effect on the current generation and shape the direction of their careers, even their lives.

Whatever our heritage, we need to recognise that change is constant, no generation is ever exactly like the last. Heraclites said 'You can't stand in the same river twice' (if you step back onto the bank just the waters flow by), which is a way of expressing how quickly things change. So isn't it better to embrace the change and bring your children up in the context of today's society rather than yesterday's, without forgetting how their family tree contributed to who they are now?

I've already made some reference to the fact that things can seem much rosier when we look back on them, so maybe now is the time to take off those rose-tinted spectacles and stamp on them. If each generation didn't push the barriers, we'd still be covering the piano legs in the way the Victorians once did. However today's children live their lives, whatever new temptations they are prone to, surely the most important thing we can teach them as single dads is a set of values as old as the hills that they can still fall back on and become functional, fulfilled and useful members of their community.

With this in mind, I've thought back to my own childhood and the things my parents taught me that have stood me in good stead in adult life. I don't pretend for a minute that I've always been able to deliver against these values but that doesn't mean I don't think they're important.

Great values to teach your kids
Don't tell lies

Is honesty the best policy? You may look around and see someone who's a bit of a 'wide boy', always got some scam on the go, he drives a 'flash motor' and seems to have plenty of spare cash. He's easy to envy but I bet my mum wouldn't have liked him.

There's a sliding scale of honesty. Most of us believe that stealing is wrong – if we didn't, the whole fabric of society would collapse – but we're more accepting of corporate theft, which, if we're being sanctimonious about it, even includes making a personal call on the company telephone. What is important is that on the really big things we're honest and if a domestic disaster occurs (chewing-gum on the carpet maybe?), I'd be much more annoyed with my children if they lied about it than if they were courageous enough to admit it.

I believe in the following adage:

> **You can't *teach* honesty without *displaying* honesty.**

You can't be selective about the way that children copy you and get a warm glow when they mimic your more endearing traits only. It's inevitable that if they catch you lying to them, they'll think it's OK to do it too. I have to say that I did come unstuck on this during The Great Santa Debate: does he exist or doesn't he? At a time when my son was facing a barrage of evidence from his peers that the famous red-clad fat fellow did not exist, he confessed to me in a conspiratorial way that he knew them to be wrong because of his certainty that 'I would never lie to him'. Well, no one's perfect.

Be polite

Saying 'Please' and 'Thank you' never did anyone any harm. Like you, I have met fawning Uriah Heep types who go over the top but if you are sincere, you will never go far wrong. One of the side-effects of living in a society that is much more 'me-focused' than ever before is that it's actually quite easy to impress people with politeness. It's such a scarce commodity that when you do use it well, you find that some folk are actually quite shocked. In business, I have always made a point of going back to the people who helped me by offering me work. After all, without them I couldn't pay the mortgage; but in our *personal* dealings it is just as powerful.

It is especially gratifying for us when someone takes time and trouble to express their thanks, so I never think it's a bad idea to get the kids to actually write to relatives who may have sent a birthday present or a few quid to supplement the DVD fund. I've encountered kids who start their sentences with 'I want...' or even worse 'Give me...' and frankly I find it offensive. 'Can I have a drink please?' is far more endearing and takes about the same time to say. Alright, if we're being strictly correct, it should be '*May* I have a drink please?' but this is a chapter about keeping their upbringing in context with the times so I think I can be forgiven.

Be considerate

If we all did unto others as we would wish them to do unto us, the world would be a much better place. Holding doors open, helping an old person with their shopping, offering a hand to a stranded motorist are a few of the many selfless acts that strangers do for each other all the time. There is no reward in this, at least not in a direct sense, but it probably helps to restore our faith in human nature and who knows, in the great circle of life you may find similar kindness offered to you in times of trouble.

When your children see you commit such acts they too will be less inclined to 'walk by on the other side' and that's a great value to teach them. Selfishness is such a horrible thing it really is gratifying to see one of your kids offer the other their last sweetie in an act of self-denial and kindness, even better if the other refuses (then *you* can eat it – only joking).

Look on the bright side

There is very little any of us can achieve by wishing that the past had been different, so it's much better to get on with the here and now and make the best of it. My dad wasn't into poetry much but he was a big fan of Omar Khayyám and bribed us to learn parts of the *Rubáiyát*, the parts that he thought were of value. My favourite, and one of the most famous passages, goes like this

The moving finger writes and having writ, moves on,
Nor all thy piety nor wit
Shall lure it back to cancel half a line,
Nor all thy tears wash out a word of it.

So, I try to impart to my children that we can learn from what's gone before but there's no point in dwelling on past failures, much better instead to see today's glass as half full. I'm a great believer in the effect of culture upon us. On a grand scale this affects us in a national sense, the British being different from the Americans or the Japanese, but I also believe you can create a microculture in those around you. Essentially, if you are all gloom and doom merchants it's hard for anyone to be happy but if each of you makes an effort to see the good things that are going on, you're far more likely to create an atmosphere of optimism.

I doubt that I am unique in having experienced the gloom, tears even, when a favourite toy has been broken. At first, I used to tell the children that it was alright and I'd repair the damage but I've learned from experience that this is not always possible. Now I simply tell them 'Everything can be fixed ... except the things that can't!' It's a kind of shorthand way of saying that there's usually a solution but even if there isn't we may as well make the best of it.

Have integrity

That sounds like a very grown-up message to be trying to impart to a child but it's not the words you use, it's the behaviours you display that will affect them from a young age. I've never met anyone who didn't suffer from some kind of insecurity, some people just mask it better than others, but it's often hard when there is peer pressure not to conform to what is going on around you. It is strange, however, in the face of the scientific fact that each of us is completely unique that we feel the need to act the same as everyone else. There are times when this is good and when we don't want to stand out in a crowd but there is also much to be said for being yourself.

Very often when we alter our behaviours on a long-term basis, to be something that someone else wants us to be, we end up miserable, simply because we lose sight of who we really are. Now I'm all for compromise (and consideration – see above) but I'm equally passionate about the need for my children to express themselves as individuals, after all this is a large part of building their self-worth. Just because 'what you see is what you get' won't please everyone, if you constantly cop out and try to live by someone else's values, *you'll* be the loser in the end.

I'd be the first to admit that I am not saintly in all I do, far from it, but if you have a value system that's worth anything, you can feel good about yourself when you do live up to it. That's an important lesson in self-esteem for us as single dads but it's just as significant if we can impart the same feelings to our children. I have an occasional email exchange with a friend of mine which is based on the Heather Small song 'Proud'. If either of us has had a good day and lived by our values, we'll send an email using the entreaty from the chorus of the song, 'What have you done today to make you feel proud?', and go on to explain some selfless action that enriched someone else's life. If you can't think of anything, it's a great way of making you resolve to do something different tomorrow.

So, what can we conclude? Lots of things have changed, but if you instil a good strong sense of values in your children, they can still live happy, rewarding, fulfilled lives and be good citizens at the same time. It's pointless to begrudge them what they have and there are two ways of looking at it; if I sometimes feel that technology is forcing them into their bedrooms to play on their computers and depriving them of the social skills so necessary to survive, at the same time I recognise that the same sort of technological breakthrough will mean that they can email me pictures of their backpacking holiday when at 19 years of age they're on the other side of the world and I'm worried sick about them. In the same way their increased wealth in monetary terms need not be a bad thing if they spend it wisely. I won't be encouraging them to salt it all away for a rainy day nor do I expect them to forego the material trappings that it will inevitably bring but I do hope they manage to save some so that with luck they'll choose a nice, comfortable, expensive retirement home for me.

Changes in values have had another effect on me too, they've made me come to realise that my own mortality isn't such a bad thing after all. If by some miracle I could double my life expectancy and carry on for a further generation, I'm sure that I'd slip from a state of being a mere grumpy old man into absolute apoplexy about the youth of the future and their lack of respect for their elders. Who knows, the shock of it may actually kill me.

The final point in this chapter is about how quickly children seem to grow up these days, which is something as parents we all lament. I don't think any of us minds them having more money or better, faster technology (most seem to be texting as soon as they can walk) but their loss of innocence at such a tender age seems unfair. Along with being more savvy and street-wise (which I think are generally good things) their time to be child-like has shortened and an alarming side-effect of this is the 'sexualisation' of children, particularly girls, before they're ready to cope with what it means.

I'm all for bringing my children up in the context of their age, not mine. I recognise they will be savvier sooner but I also think it is part of my duty of care to let them, encourage them even, to be children for as long as they can.

PRACTICAL

6

A man's work is never done

If you look back at how your gran ran her household, there's no excuse for us not being able to cope. With none of the advantages of modern technology to save her labour, she still managed to run the whole thing like clockwork. Why? Because she had a *system*. You need one too.

Whether you pride yourself on being pristine or are satisfied with being a slob is of no importance because regardless of your preference, the kids can't be scruffy or smelly or hungry or over-tired without other people noticing. And the last thing they want is to be noticed, except when it's of their choosing.

Children are hugely tolerant of all sorts of situations but their basic needs have to be met. I've found that the better I do this, the closer I feel to them. I also think they feel more calm and secure; after all, what could be worse than seeing your dad struggling with the fundamental basics of looking after you? Coping is not only important for your self-esteem but an essential part of letting the children know that just because you're a single dad the world isn't falling apart. I don't care for my kids through guilt, I do it because I want to. Perhaps it's because they're not with me all the time that I feel the least I can do is to look after them properly when they are.

There's a big difference between *nurturing* them and *spoiling* them, a great gulf between their independence and your neglect. Great dads do their best to teach kids how to do stuff for themselves, but *until* they've learned we have to be prepared to do it for them. We're lucky though, more of us than ever before have lived on our own at some time and had to cope with the chores. Looking after the kids is pretty much an extension of that, so read on for practical tips on health, hygiene, bath-time, bedtime and bonding.

Squeaky clean

You don't have to follow the regime they're used to at their mum's but you do need to create one of your own and stick to it. As with all these domestic issues, routine is a great thing, because then the children will know to expect what's coming and it will no longer be a cause for argument or debate.

Chucking them in the bath at the end of each day is a real winner on many fronts. It tends to have a calming effect and once they're out and dry, hey presto!, the next step is pyjamas/nightie and that sounds to me like one small step away from bedtime. Tiny tots need your full attention and a good sponging down, but as they get older they'll do this themselves. Some supervision is still required for quite some time as kids have a tendency to just soak aimlessly and miss doing the important bits.

Our bath-time ritual usually involves me sitting on the loo seat and having a chat about the day just been, the state of the universe or the significance of global brands in an increasingly competitive economy. No, honest, I never cease to be amazed at what they'll take on when I have their full attention. This is also the time of day when I start to unwind, so it's not unknown for me to indulge in this exercise with a beer in my hand. I'm sure it helps me make more sense too.

It's a great place for them to unload as well because they soon realise that for once you really *are* listening (instead of occasionally interjecting with a well-timed 'Uh-huh'), so they may want to tell you about the latest bust-up with one of their mates or how mummy's boyfriend sometimes says rude words.

Try to make the most of this ritual because it will soon pass and will be replaced by the teen years when you will not only miss seeing them splash about in the bath but will miss seeing the inside of your bathroom for hours, even days, on end.

I'm pretty keen on this theme of how our task as fathers is to help our children grow away from us a little bit more each day; to add an increment of independence as every unit of time passes. This applies as much to personal hygiene as anything else. Newborn babies smell lovely, their aroma evokes the very soul of Mother Nature herself, but it's all downhill from there. By the time they reach early teens, they smell horrible if you're not careful.

When the time comes, help them through the transition. Spend time in Boot's explaining what does what, then let them pick the most heavily advertised stuff.

The laundry man

Keeping the kids smelling sweet is one thing but it doesn't stop there. You also need to make sure they've got clean clothes, which either means relying on them being sent with sufficient outfits to last the duration of their stay or the timely and judicious use of the washing machine.

Fortunately, I made all my laundry gaffes long ago, turning all my underwear pink with the help of that bright red T-shirt I got in the market or shrinking stuff to the kind of proportions that would fit a doll or action figure, so, to date, I've managed to avoid doing the same with the kids' clothes. It always fascinates me why the average automatic washing machine has so many settings; I've only ever used two. Maybe one day I'll get the instruction book out again and find out what all the others are for.

My only rules (and the secret of my success) are to keep light and dark stuff apart and allow the scientific miracles contained in the washing powder to do the work, rather than rely on scalding hot water. If stuff doesn't come out clean enough, I just wash it again and turn the temperature up a bit. I've also found it's not a good idea to overfill the machine as then nothing really comes out very clean.

Increasingly, we're getting to the stage in our house where there are some favourite clothes and by this I mean they need to be surgically removed at bedtime, safe in the knowledge that they'll be put on again tomorrow and the next day and the next...

In these circumstances it helps if you put them straight in the washing machine when they're taken off, then get them out the instant the programme has finished and hang them up to dry or get them over a radiator. That way they should be ready for the morning, smelling fresh and sweet.

A few other things: my past disasters have led me to learn that really delicate things are best washed by hand in soap flakes (which make your hands feel all soft!) and that stuff like grass stains can only be shifted by a bit of pre-soaking in a bucket with a suitable proprietary product.

If you're going on holiday, you can get a handy-sized tube of liquid 'travel wash', which, while it might seem a bit too organised and verging towards the 'anal', may just save your life, particularly if you've got younger kids who can get through half a dozen outfits in a day.

Washing is easy and drying is a breeze. In summer 'hang on line', in winter 'put in tumble dryer' if you have one; if not, then adorn your radiators but don't let the stuff that has to be ironed get too dry or it's a nightmare. Remember too to remove all the underwear before you bring your latest hot date back for coffee (I mean the underwear on the radiators, not the ones you're wearing, on second thoughts ...).

Top Tip If you're hanging out the world's largest collection of socks, just bung them up any old how. When they're dry and you're taking them off, pick them out in pairs so you don't have all the faff of doing it later. Even

Fab free family fun time

Here's a game that's a great laugh, completely cost neutral and carries almost no risk of injury at all, yes, it's Sock Wars. The name is obviously a parody of *Star Wars* but that is where the similarity ends, unless you want to be really daft and dress as Darth Vadar.

Sock Wars involves you throwing rolled-up pairs of socks at each other. It's best if you can each have a territory (either end of the room) with maybe a sofa or something to hide behind, before you appear fully loaded and unleash hell upon each other. A 'below head height' rule is good if you want to stop ornaments being knocked off things and as this is a game that often follows the wash cycle, but before the 'putting away' stage has happened, I find it is enhanced by the wearing of a pair of protective underpants on the head. (In fact they afford no protection whatever but it does make the game funnier.) If you have more than one child, you have to balance up the odds and make sure that you attack each with equal force or they'll feel picked on. You may also expect that they won't be nearly so fair minded, forming an immediate alliance to bring the collective might of their forces down upon you. Take it in good part, after all they're only socks.

little kids can help here – get them to roll the socks into balls before you put them away. It's a simple skill and you'll get away with it if you tell them it's good for the soul.

Ironing is a rather trickier skill but most blokes can do it these days so I'm not going to patronise you. If you find it a bore, then I can offer some advice to jazz it up. Unlike the American president who reputedly couldn't walk and chew gum at the same time, I think for us single dads *three* tasks at once is eminently achievable.

I can iron, watch 'MOTD' and drink a beer at the same time. If I go as far as recommending this to you, I might find myself in hot water with the Health and Safety Executive, so I'll just leave it at saying I can do it, so there. (Try not to get confused and fill the steam iron with beer or all your clothes will end up smelling like a brewery.)

Suffice to say, only iron the stuff you really have to. Frankly, if I got knocked down I'd be chuffed to arrive in hospital with *clean* undies, let alone pressed! If I have to prioritise the ironing, because I have much more impor- tant things to do with my time, then I do the kids' stuff first. This is based on the premise that I don't much care what people think of how I look but would be mortified if they took stick because I let them go out looking like an unmade bed (even if it meant I could enter them for the Turner prize).

Tidiness and cleanliness

I hold my hands up and admit that I can live in a bit of a mess and as I don't have a dust allergy I'm usually quite happy to co-exist with a fair amount of it. Occasionally it gets to me and I have to blitz the place, putting me (albeit temporarily) into the unusual category of tidy, fastidious heterosexual male.

Being untidy is one thing but being unclean is a completely different kettle of fish. On that basis, let's look at the areas of the house that are really important.

Kitchens, bathrooms and bacteria

I don't care how much of a slob you are, this bit (part of the cleanliness and tidiness thing) is something I feel really strongly about because getting it wrong can literally have dire consequences for your children.

Even if the rest of the house is a mess, I like to think that the kitchen and bathroom are clean. Without going into too muh detail, be hygienic! Although you're often living like a bachelor, resist the temptation to live in a 'bachelor pad'. You might want to gamble with your health when it comes to food hygiene but always remember that your kids will often be involved now. Get into the habit of doing the sort of thing I suspect they're always going on about in *Good Housekeeping* magazine, e.g. in the fridge store cooked and raw meat separately, and with the raw *below* the cooked (in case of drips).

Wash up a little and often rather than saving it up for a week and indulging yourself in binge cleaning. This stops the bits of leftover food hosting their very own bacteria sleepover where they invite any passing staphylococci to come and stay a while.

I hate washing-up so I've made a rule that I can't start it until I've cleared the draining board of the last lot (which I usually do while I'm running the water for the next lot!), at least I've then got some space to work in.

When it comes to drying the dishes – maybe it's a man thing – I just don't see the point. Of all the household chores that need doing, count off on your fingers, right now, the number that will do themselves if you leave them. Do the beds make themselves? I think not. Does the hoover work on its own? Not when I'm looking it doesn't. And yet, by the miracle of nature, the dishes dry themselves, so why keep a dog and bark yourself. If you do catch yourself doing the drying while you idly gaze out of the kitchen window, it really is time to consider if you're getting out enough.

Bins are interesting, especially kitchen bins. Remember when you were married, one of your primary uses, other than getting the lids off recalcitrant jars, was to 'do the bins'. This will stand you in good stead now. However, it's not the *doing* of the bins that is the issue but the *frequency*. Your former partner would probably have been responsible for instructing you on this but now another helpful female will advise you, Mother Nature, for it is she who is responsible for the rotting of the food scraps which causes that smell that tells you it is time to change the bin-bag. This might all seem a bit obvious but if you live on your own a lot of the time it can take a week to fill a bin, by which time it's probably pretty stinky. Apart from the off-putting smell, this is also a health hazard in the kitchen, so change it often.

At the risk of sounding forward, let's move upstairs. The bathroom is the second primary venue for bacteria and I don't really want to go into its sources; you can work that out for yourself. However, you can minimise this by keeping the bath, sink and especially toilet squeaky clean. For the latter, bleach is great but you need to squirt it in and leave it a while for it to do its job (that's after you've done yours) so it's better, if you've got young ones, to do it while they're asleep to avoid the risk of them coming into contact with it.

Bath and sink cleaners now come in many forms; the easiest is the foam stuff. You just spray it on, leave it for a nanosecond and rinse it off, along with the accumulated gunge. As an extra plus, if you run out of shaving foam you can always use a squirt of this as an alternative (only joking). All of these things are simply a part of sensible personal hygiene and if you don't teach your children by example, how will they ever learn how important they are?

yum yum, it's tea-time

The food thing is really important. I don't have a selection of recipes for you to follow but I do feel really strongly that food has become an issue these days and we have a very serious parental responsibility to get it right. Just as the TV has an off switch, so that you can regulate what they watch (when you're feeling brave enough), so too does the fridge in a metaphorical sense. Up to a certain age kids can only consume what's in the house and if you're doing the food shopping, you can control their intake at source, as it were.

Ironically, it is the power of TV which has not only persuaded a generation to eat more junk but has also raised awareness of the consequential increase in child obesity. Consuming fewer Turkley Twizzler adverts and more Jamie Oliver documentaries is a much healthier diet for our children.

I'm neither a dietitian nor a health food freak and I think there are times when only a double bacon cheeseburger with fries can hit the spot, but generally there is too much saturated fat and sugar in our diet and the result is all around us in the alarming rates of obesity that threaten the health of our own children and the eating habits of future generations. I don't want to be a crashing bore or Goody Two Shoes, but it's all about balance.

Try to get lots of fresh fruit and veg down them (it's just as convenient as so-called convenience food), make treats like chocolate exactly that, something special, not part of the daily routine intake, and try to get some meal times in place rather than succumbing to a culture of grazing all day long.

I was once invited to a presentation by an airline company so that they could show off their new long-haul experience. Yes, the new seats, extra legroom and personal movie screens were impressive, but they were just as proud of their new food regime, which they'd branded 'snack attack'. It seemed that if the regular meals, served at about 15-minute intervals throughout the duration of the 10-hour flight, weren't enough, you could press a buzzer and have one of the cabin crew bring you an extra portion of deep-fried, sugar-coated, battered lard to keep you going. If there are too many 'snack attacks' happening in your house, then take some positive action.

When it comes to the 'occasion' of dining, there's a lot of bollocks talked nowadays. Although my mum would be ashamed of me because I don't even possess a tablecloth, it doesn't stop us all eating together. Mostly we sit at the breakfast bar in the kitchen, all in a row like in an American diner, but at least we're sharing food as a family – the meal is an occasion, of sorts, and the kids still have to ask permission before they get down. I know it's a weird combination of old-fashioned values and modern informality but it works for us.

I do heartily recommend the proper family meal from time to time. In winter we do it for Sunday lunch and it's become something of a ritual, with both children mucking in to help prepare it. This sometimes results in mini-sprouts as they compete to see how many layers they can peel off without the things disintegrating altogether. They seem to genuinely enjoy the whole experience and, as with the revelations of bath-time (see above), you'll be amazed what you can learn when you have a conversation that's not competing with the usual screen-based entertainments.

I've decided to add something to this section on how to cook, not the ingredients and method – Delia is far better at all that than I am – but simply a basic rule on how to make food safe. Taking it as read that you've been prepared to have a kitchen and food hygiene regimen, all of this will be but a house of cards if you don't cook food thoroughly. Veg and stuff is pretty safe anyway but as Morrissey once said 'Meat is murder'. Again, under most circumstances, if you follow the recommended cooking times and temperatures, you'll be OK, but grilling and frying, both of which can generate lots of heat, can be more tricky as you may risk cooking the stuff on the outside but leaving the inside raw and dangerous. I think the phrase 'always ensure food is piping hot' just about sums this up.

The time when you face greatest danger is the summer, partly because in warm weather everything deteriorates more quickly, especially if you haven't kept it refrigerated, but mostly due to the British male's modern predilection to barbecue. This practice is made even more dangerous by the fact that it's not just preferable but virtually compulsory to have a beer in your hand while you do it. Research carried out at The Theo Institute for Made-Up Studies shows that the risk of food poisoning is directly proportional to the number of beers consumed.

Furthermore, the risks to your children are increased many-fold by the fact that you will always light a barbecue about an hour after you should have done, forgetting from last time (only a few days before) that they take forever to get up to cooking heat. This will ensure that your offspring will be close to starvation by the time you serve up, meaning that (a) you will hurry the process and give them food that isn't properly cooked, and (b) they will consume a greater than average quantity of the bacteria-ridden stuff in an attempt to satisfy their hunger.

Fathers are much more likely to inflict this on their children for the simple reason that lighting a barbecue is such a man thing. With those caveman days of hunting wild beasts armed only with a piece of twig adorned with a tip of flint now far behind us, we can only truly revert to our natural instincts by 'making fire'. It's as if the whole question of our sexuality rests on our ability to nuke half a dozen beefburgers. Personally I've always been a bit of a failure on this front, as I could never get the damned thing to stay lit (a mate did recommend his personal method, which I recall was based on a gallon of Four Star and a match).

Barbecueing skills may nevertheless be hereditary, with my brother inheriting our family's entire gene set to my detriment. He could best be described as a 'serial barbecuer' and every year he fed his obsession by going out and buying a new one. He started with the conventional charcoal kettle barbecue, moved on to a gas-powered one and I think he now owns one fuelled by nuclear technology.

I should point out though that this wasn't something my dad was particularly proud of, he used to call me and say they'd been invited to my brother's on Sunday, for more of the 'black food'.

But I'm digressing. If you don't want to get ill from food alfresco, the best thing to do is cook it all in the oven first, waft it with a flourish over the hot charcoal and serve immediately, garnished with two Imodium.

Up the wooden hill

That's what my mum used to say to me when it was time for bed. I yearned to live in a lighthouse because then I could argue that as the steps were stone, I didn't need to go, at which mum would probably have used another of her expressions that's not printable here.

Bedtime is for you as much as them. What I mean is that there are benefits to be had all round, although it is harder to see what they might be from where the kids are viewing it. They simply feel like they're being banished to the bedroom, just as the really good stuff is coming on telly. Bedtime can be fun – read to them or sing to them.

I don't think there are any rules that state the time at which children should be in bed; it's for you to gauge. It's a lot simpler if your kids are close in age because then there's one bedtime for all of them and you don't suffer the drawn-out agony of negotiating with each one as the appointed hour (or minute or second) arrives.

Here are some things that may help you decide when the right time is.

- *Have you had enough of them? Even though you love them so, you're entitled to some time to yourself.*
- *Do they look exhausted but refuse to admit it?*
- *Is it term-time? They usually need more sleep when they're at school.*
- *Do you owe them a treat, by letting them stay up late 'just tonight'?*
- *Do they find it hard to concentrate on the matter in hand (homework, requests from you, etc.)?*
- *Are they horrible in the daytime, as a result of having too little sleep last night?*

The last point is an important one; you may let your kids stay up late for a whole load of reasons but if they're naturally early risers, you will probably pay the price the next day, with an increase in tetchiness all round. I know a bloke who deliberately used to keep the kids up late the night before they went back to their mother just so she would suffer the fallout. Disgraceful!

I started this chapter by stating the importance of having a system, a routine if you like, so I hope that some of the things I've recommended help you get in the swing of that. Believe me, it helps preserve your sanity and reduce your stress with the added benefit that you 'manage the expectation' of your children. I think that this is one of the secrets of being a great dad. If you promise them the moon and the stars and then deliver an overcast night with a light drizzle, they are going to be disappointed.

I can still remember desperately wanting a pet monkey when I was four years old. Preposterous, I know, but it seemed like a good idea at the time. Relentless badgering (come to think of it, a badger might have made a better pet) led Mum and Dad to offer that distant promise all parents succumb to from time to time, 'Well, maybe one day ...' I bet that once I'd grown up, if I asked either of them, they'd struggle to remember saying that but kids have memories like elephants (maybe an elephant would have been more practical) when it comes to these things and, yes, I'm still waiting, still monkey-less, still hopeful.

I learned my lesson the hard way –

don't promise what you can't deliver

So the practical aspects of looking after the household don't have to be a chore (or a series of chores) as long as you keep ahead of the game. The biggest benefit is that the better organised you are, the more time you'll have to spend with the kids, doing the things that matter, the fun things, which gets us all closer to our goal of greatness.

7

I haven't got a thing to wear

Clothes are really important to kids and as each year goes by, they'll take more and more interest in what they wear. We shouldn't underestimate the social significance of how we dress and that's because we're all guilty of the same crime of judging a book by its cover. Which clothes you choose to wear says so much about you to other people, it's one of the earliest indicators of personality to those you meet, even before you've opened your mouth or had a chance to give yourself away with body language. Children are quick to learn this trick as well and it won't be long before they're making judgements about others based on their threads.

It's also the case that as a society we use clothing to indicate the status of an occasion or the level of formality of a gathering of peers. Blokes meeting each other in the pub seldom make much effort to dress up, whereas for 'ladies who lunch' the outfit they select can make or break the occasion. Making the differentiation between idiosyncratic style and conforming to accepted protocols can be tough. You're brave if you attend an interview in jeans and T-shirt but if you were applying for a job as a graphic artist, it might be entirely appropriate.

Because of the subtleties and nuances of this 'game', it's our duty to make sure we don't have our children singled out, simply because *we* might choose not to fit in with the norm. I'm not saying we should follow a lowest common denominator kind of dress code, just that it's something to think about before you expose your kids to a cruel world.

Aside from the issue of style there are lots of practical considerations to be addressed and at a basic level you need to make sure your children are appropriately dressed for the weather. By the age of 10 or 12 the clothing debate will be taken out of your hands. As they start to decide for themselves what's in and what's out, it's more likely that your contribution will just be in the form of cash taken out of your wallet.

Estranged couples I know have a 'blended approach' to the issue of clothing. That means you both have some stock of suitable attire on the understanding that individual items transfer from one home to another on a regular, if hit and miss, basis. Having two complete and distinct wardrobes is beyond the means of most people, so you have to have some negotiation and cooperation over what goes where and when.

The level of difficulty of managing this really depends on the items of clothing under discussion. You shouldn't have too much trouble with socks and underwear, as these are relatively low-cost items and you can afford to have a drawer full at each venue. We have suffered the odd knicker crisis where everything has seemed to be at mum's, but a regular stock check can prevent it. It's also worth checking the labels now and again. I once discovered underpants for kids aged five to six in my lad's drawer and as he's now 12 I did think they might be getting just a tad tight; still, it'll stop his voice breaking.

Although the cost gets greater for other items, you can shop for cheap T-shirts and jeans or leggings that might only get worn when everything else is in the wash – a kind of emergency kit, if you like. The quality may not be great but because kids grow so quickly they're unlikely to wear them out. All of this avoids the unnecessary crisis of really having nothing to wear.

Once you've got these items as a base, you can hopefully reach the stage where their better clothes move with them and if you only have the children with you at weekends, you don't need a huge amount at any one time. This changes a bit when it comes to holiday time and the kids are going to be with you for maybe a fortnight. I pick up a bagful of suitable items when I collect them and try to be charitable enough to take the majority back clean, if not ironed, a day or two after they've returned.

I've got a great story about inappropriate clothing later but before first let me issue a warning specifically about underwear. When we were small, we went to stay with family friends in north Wales. Such was the success of the visit that we decided to prolong it by a day or two, meaning that my mum (usually meticulously well planned) didn't have enough clean undies for me. Now, I was only about three at the time and as our friends had a daughter of a similar age the easiest thing was for me to wear a pair of her freshly laundered smalls. Both mums did everything to convince me that these were the same as my own (and in terms of the look of them it was hard to argue), yet even at this tender age I was uncomfortable and deeply embarrassed about the whole affair. Perish the thought if the same thing happened now, I mean exactly which side does a chap dress when he's wearing a thong and as for that stringy bit that goes up the back, I can only imagine that when you move it's like flossing your rear end. The moral of the story is that if kids really don't want to wear what you've chosen for them, don't force the issue.

Emergency items

There are a few things in the clothing line that I think are essential to have in stock, only because the frequency of their use is so sporadic that you can guarantee they'll be in the wrong house at the wrong time. This includes swimming kit, again relatively inexpensive and nicely stretchy, so they can still get into it years after you bought it.

Wellies too are a great thing to have lying around, an item of infrequent use in any household, they're normally grown out of before you wear them out, which means you might be able to blag some from a relative or friend whose kids are older or find something suitable and cheap in a charity shop. Hats, gloves and something waterproof also fit into this category and we're not talking about dressing them in Sunday best here, just if you want to slob about in the garden or if a bit of unexpected snow arrives and you want to take full advantage.

Shopping for clothes: some basic tips

Most blokes I know hate shopping for their own clothes, so the experience of doing it for your children isn't exactly going to fill you with joy. However, you can make it slightly less painful if you follow some easy ground rules. As I've said, up to a certain age you can have control over what they wear but it does get harder as they become more fashion-conscious. When that time comes, you'll go through a phase of having to give them a greater say when they're stopping with you but it doesn't last long as they'll soon be heading off for town with their own clothing agenda. I don't want to start sexual stereotyping here but in my experience the whole clothing issue is much greater for girls; boys just seem to care less about what they wear. Anyway, for what it's worth here's my advice ...

Fly solo

If clothes shopping is a chore, it's made all the worse by dragging reluctant little mannequins around with you, asking them if they prefer the pink or the taupe. I'd much rather scoop up an armful of stuff and allow them a try-on session at home. This seems to work much better, particularly if you don't interrupt an episode of 'Sponge Bob' to do it. On your own you're much more nimble and if you've got any sense, you'll do the whole thing in a single shop, thereby reducing the pain.

Shop local

There's a really good reason for this. If I find a selection of gear but can't come to a decision which to buy, I stick the whole lot on a credit card and then let the kids choose. This is really only a practical strategy if you can return the unwanted stuff to the shop in short order so that they can put the refund directly on your card before you've had to shell out for it in real money. The only risk with this is that the kids might like everything you've bought but if so, then what the hell.

Choose chains

Big stores are good when it comes to taking stuff back, they rarely argue, but don't dismiss a good local independent trader out of hand, just make sure they're happy to refund you if the items you've chosen don't fit. Personally I hate taking stuff back, it seems like such an affront, but it's better than having a wardrobe full of unwearable items. One local chain store I use for my own clothing has a policy of asking for a reason for the return. Usually if you grunt 'Wrong size', they're happy to issue the credit but last time I returned something I couldn't resist stating the reason as 'Frankly I look a bit of a git in this', just to see if they'd put it on their form.

Size them up

Most mass-produced clothing is pretty accurate in sizing items according to the age of the child but kids do grow at different rates, so this is not always a reliable measure. I get hugely irritated when it only states the size in centimetres – I couldn't hope to guess at the height of my kids in feet and inches let alone in some foreign currency. Still, all this can be avoided if you take a peek at the label of something they're currently wearing, which seems, in some vague way, to fit them.

Fashion-conscious

I tend to shy away from anything too outlandish, knowing as I do that until they reach the age of self-expression (and will therefore only wear black) children don't want to stand out as being a bit 'wacky'. (This I know from personal experience, as I describe later in the story about the oilskins!)

Practicalities

Shy away from anything that is complicated to do up, it'll only take you longer to dress the kids in the morning and their chances of mastering some button/zip/Velcro combo at an early age are much reduced in comparison to a sweatshirt that slips over their heads. At the same time think about the washing and ironing implications of what you're buying and read the labels before you get to the till to make sure you're not making more work for yourself further down the line.

Asexual apparel

If you've got more than one child and they're of different sexes, it may be that you'll think carefully about some of the items you buy (like T-shirts and jogging bottoms, for example) because they can be worn by either sex at a push. I still think it's better if each child feels a sense of ownership for their stuff but if you've run out of clean clothes, a selection that fits into the his 'n' hers category could prove useful.

Avoid designer labels

It's just a personal thing but I really don't believe in parading my kids around in advertisements for some French fashion house. There are loads of really good makes that are practical and stylish without falling into the high-fashion trap. Anyway, you can be secure in the knowledge that peer pressure will soon bring them into line on the designer scene and they'd rather die than be seen in anything from the supermarket.

Hand-me-downs

A generation ago, if you were the youngest child in the family, you spent most of your life wearing the clothes of your older siblings. This was no surprise when the nation was less affluent and most kids out-grew before they wore out their clothes. Although it's less prevalent now, I'm never sniffy if someone offers me clothing for the children, as long as it fits and doesn't look ridiculous, it's fine by me. I mentioned charity shops before and if you're on a budget, they're a really good place to shop. Equally, things like the school Christmas fair or local scouts jumble sale can yield some great bargains. Don't be too proud to give it a go.

Shoes

I've saved a separate section for shoe buying because of the consequences of getting it wrong. Big baggy sweatshirts, or jeans that are a bit on the tight side, won't make much material difference in the long run but the wrong-fitting shoes can damage young feet.

It's more expensive to go to a reputable high street store and have their feet measured properly but it's worth the investment. Keeping it all in the family, we went to the shop my nephew works at during his holidays from university and got him to do the job (we also prevailed upon his staff discount, good scam, eh!). In fairness to the lad he's been really well trained and showed us the different ways of ensuring that the shoes fitted properly (this was after doing meticulous measurements of the feet before selecting carefully from the stock room). Press down here, slide your little finger in there, it was all very professional. When he asked my little girl to stand on one leg and whistle 'Dixie', I did think he'd perhaps gone too far. Fair play though, the shoes fit like a dream.

My only exception to this high street rule is for holiday shoes, where a cheap pair 'down-the-market' are ideal as long as they're not to be worn all day every day. 'Jelly shoes', canvas ones or sandals are great for slobbing about the beach in but check back regularly on the first day of wear to make sure that their little feet aren't getting sore. Because of the rate of kids' growth you'll only get a season out of them but if they were cheap in the first place, you can bin them when you get home.

caring for clothes

I've tried to stress the importance of low-maintenance clothes simply because I'd rather be playing with the kids than ironing their outfits. I think it's a good idea to teach them from an early age that they have a duty of care with their togs too, so when they get undressed for the bath, I ask them to sort out what needs washing and put it in the linen basket and make some attempt to fold and put away the others. It doesn't really matter if they make a hash of it, the principle is the thing.

If my two forget, I only have to mention the TK Maxx bag and instantly they are galvanised into action. This is because in the early days when the divorce settlement was not even signed, I discovered that I had not got custody of the linen basket so we were forced to use the aforementioned carrier from a local boutique. In these more affluent days in the Theobald household we now have our very own fit-for-the-purpose dirty linen basket but it will forever more be known as the TK Maxx bag.

It's best not to leave stuff festering in there for too long, as it will start to rise up and plot against you. By now you should know the form with the washing machine: little and often is better than the world's biggest wash in a single load.

Taking good care of clothes should give them a good chance of surviving the course, so as I've said before, it is more likely that the children will grow out of them before they're full of holes (the clothes that is, not the children). If they're in reasonable nick, I wash and iron them, then take them to the Oxfam shop. Funny how when they were being worn by my own children I cared less about the odd crease but if they're destined for the developing world I'd be mortified to think I'd sent something un-ironed.

So, they're my Top Tips, just work out what's good for you and follow your instinct. But before you do, read this final salutary tale, which might just influence your choices. I really do think it's true that up to a certain age you can get kids to wear most things, especially if you enthuse about how they look in them during the trying-on session. However, there are times when you can overstep the mark and just such an incident happened in our household many years ago.

We were living in Scotland at the time and I would have been around five years old, my brother about seven and sister ten. Due to the inclement weather conditions that prevail in that part of the world (it pissed down for the whole two years we were there), my folks decided to invest in some appropriate apparel and took us to God-knows-what-kind of store in town to buy coats. We came away with ... wait for it ... bright yellow oilskins. Sadly this is only the half of it. Yes, we really had taken leave of our senses when we purchased the matching pointy sou'wester hats. Looking back I can only imagine my dad was some kind of magician who had cast a spell over us so that we actually thought we looked good in them. Sadly for him, the hex didn't last long, so on Monday morning when we were kitted out ready for school it suddenly dawned on us that we looked like refugees from the North Sea Academy of Fishing. Tears and tantrums followed but eventually we calmed Dad down and explained that we wouldn't be setting foot outside the house in this ridiculous get-up. Now if that tale doesn't influence your clothes-buying habits, I don't know what will.

8

High days and holidays

Ever feel like you need a break? I know I do and although it's a very different game when you take the children it can be very therapeutic indeed, if you plan it right. When you're holding down a full-time job, you probably get only four or five weeks' paid holiday a year, so because it's in short supply, you really need to make the best of it. For the sake of your sanity you should try to get some time away by yourself, I mean without the kids, but if possible save the lion's share to spend with them.

Just a few days away on a long weekend can be enough to recharge your batteries and because time seems to pass so slowly when you're younger, it's good if you can plan some shorter trips in between the main events. The change of scene can be really valuable and it might only involve going to stay with family or friends for a day or two.

If part of what we do as parents is create memories for our children, holidays are a fantastic way of doing this in a condensed way. When I think back to my own childhood, I don't remember much about the day-to-day stuff but I can recall us all playing rounders on a beach somewhere. It seemed like I hadn't a care in the world and come to think of it I probably hadn't.

All of us recognise how daily life can become a matter of routine: we get up each morning and set off for work, do what has to be done and come home again, but it's very easy for the children's time with you to be a bit repetitive too. Most of us spend part of the weekend ferrying them from some activity or another (football, swimming lessons, ballet, whatever) and though it's a break from school for them, it's hardly riveting stuff. During all this rushing about we get very little time to really interact with each other. Spend a week or two away with the kids and you'll be amazed at how much better you get to know them and vice versa. Aside from that, if you get it right, it's bloody good fun!

Holidays *should* be a great way of relieving stress but this isn't always the case – delays at airports, tummy bugs and the host of other 'little accidents' that can happen might make you return home in need of a good break. However, most of this can be avoided or certainly lessened if you plan your holiday properly.

I won't presume to tell you where to go or what to do. Apart from anything else, I don't consider myself to have a particularly adventurous spirit, so what may suit me and mine may just bore you and yours. It's for you to decide and the first criterion you should apply to selecting where to go is your personal preference, yours and the kids': what is it you like to do together? Next, take into account physical factors, like how many children you are taking and will there be other adults in your party who can help out? What ages are your kids? If they're very young, you might decide that a long-haul flight is out of the question. Try to pick a location that's got something for everyone, where the kids will be entertained and have fun and you won't be left counting the hours until you return. Not all the factors will be within your control, and budget is a critical one here. You will be limited by what you can afford. For most of us we have to do some kind of balancing act with the cash but I came to realise some time ago how quickly the children grow up and if you're waiting until you're 'flush with dosh' before you set off on the 'big spectacular', you may find they've grown beyond it without you noticing. If you're wondering whether to change the car this year, have a conservatory built or go on a really good holiday, I think there's no contest. Like I said, you're making memories here and I hardly think they'll look back with affection in their adult lives and say 'Do you remember the summer when dad had that really lovely conservatory built?'

Finally, one of the things that come pretty high on my list is the 'hassle factor' and the amount of influence I have over it. On my own I might set off for foreign climes, expecting to sort out some accommodation when I get there, but I'd never do it with the children. Where possible I try to cover as many contingencies in advance so that all they have to worry about is having a good time.

I promised not to instruct you on where you should go

but I did think it would be worth listing some of the things that, generally speaking, children enjoy, even if only to spark your own thoughts. Happy memories for me include some of the following:

- beaches
- exploring
- adventure
- activities
- swimming
- cycling
- walking
- castles
- theme parks
- camping
- sightseeing

A few words about some of these. I'm continually astounded by the amount of time that children can amuse themselves for on a beach. Me and a mate of mine took our collected total of five children to one once and they played all day. The fact that it was a beach with a pub on it did help to influence our choice but remember to always drink responsibly, just like we did. There's something very therapeutic about sand and sea (and beer) and you can always get into competitive sand-castle building with the 'smug-married' dads around you.

What might seem like a fairly mundane day out to you can soon be turned into action and adventure if you can spark the children's imagination. When they're old enough, it's hard to beat a good game of hide-and-seek in the woods. Castles and sightseeing can be fun too but don't overdo it – try to limit this to half a day at a time or they'll get bored. I've put camping in because we do it one weekend a year with friends and though I hate that business of sleeping on a thin strip of foam that does little to mitigate against the bumpy ground, the children love it, so I figure a bit of self-sacrifice once in a while doesn't do any harm.

I come to this last point about the camping trips because the friends we always go with have children of similar ages and if there's one thing that will amuse your children for hours, it's other children. Even if you're not setting off as a big party, choose somewhere that other families go to so that new friends can be found and made. Not only is this really good for your kids but it also gives you a bit of a break from having to entertain them during every waking hour.

When it comes to keeping them amused, it's really good to go somewhere that has organised activities.

The old-style holiday camps are hard to beat if you're looking for wall-to-wall fun.

The other great thing about them is that you can choose something active like go-kart rides, or a passive pursuit like watching a show (shows go on virtually all day every day). It's a really good way of coping with the oscillating energy levels of youngsters.

Types of accommodation

Under canvas is basic but good fun and cheap, the only downside, unless you're prepared to do all that campfire cooking, is that you need to eat out a lot, so that can put the cost up. You'll certainly return home knowing you've been on an adventure and if you choose the same weekend in July that we always do, you can be guaranteed rain.

A tent and the gear that goes with it is a good investment if you're committed to using it for a number of years but if not, you may choose a site where they're already set up with all the necessary equipment as part of the package. The French are very big on this, with the added bonus that rain is less likely.

Self-catering accommodation covers a multitude of sins but it has the benefit of being a bit more permanent and can provide a good base for your other activities. The main plus here is that you can please yourselves on meal times and on what you eat. It does mean more effort in shopping for and preparing food but the freedom it gives you is not a bad trade-off in my book. Most self-catering accommodation has reasonable cooking facilities and you don't have to traipse across the campsite to the wash block to clean up afterwards.

Hotels tend to cost more, but you have to think less about what to take as it's all on site. Of course, the standards vary widely and when you've got children with you, it's best if you can either get a small and friendly family hotel that's been recommended or a reputable chain where what you see (probably on the Internet) is what you get. Most hotels are now priced per room/per night so you pay a fixed rate regardless of how many you have kipping down. The budget hotel chains usually offer 'family rooms', some sleeping as many as five, so you can all bunk in together. This is obviously essential if the children are very young but even as they grow up a bit, they like the security of having you around, especially if you're in a strange environment.

Planning

Why not start with sorting out some dates? If you've got a reasonable relationship with your ex-partner, it will help you negotiate some flexibility on when you go away. With school-age children that six-week summer holiday should allow you sufficient leeway to get a suitable break organised but if their time with you is set in stone, it's much more difficult to get the holiday you want. If possible try to agree on the *length* rather than the *specific date* of the holiday and promise to get it booked early so that everyone knows where they stand.

The next thing to do is to decide where or at least what *kind* of place you're going to go. Think carefully about the implications of this. If you choose to stay in Blighty, the weather may be less good but you'll have a greater deal of control over possible glitches; apart from anything else you won't have to deal with language barriers. Having said that, there's a real bonus in going abroad as you come back feeling like you've had a proper break. Many resorts these days have a very laid-back atmosphere and if you choose somewhere mainstream, most of the locals will speak some English and you'll be able to get by. On the up-side you're more likely to get good weather – you shouldn't underestimate how difficult it can be to keep the kids amused during a fortnight of downpours.

Wherever possible, try to find someone you trust who will give you a personal recommendation. This can save you a lot of hassle as you'll know the best places to shop, eat or be entertained, they'll recommend the best beaches and tell you what to look out for if you're hiring a car. Most of us only go to any one place the one time and it can be frustrating if you spent the entire break sussing out the best way of enjoying it when you should have been just enjoying it. It's worth checking at this point that the resort you're about to book is a family one rather than a cesspit of boozed-up teenagers out to get laid.

The Internet can be a great place to start searching but do be aware that it's easy to make things look better than they are. After all, the sites you visit are only acting like an online brochure, which can be just as deceptive as the printed version. The other difficulty with the Internet is that it tends to be unregulated, so choosing a company you've heard of that has the necessary ABTA or AITO accreditation is my strong recommendation. Also, if you're afraid you'll be abandoned when you arrive, check that there's a local holiday company representative who can resolve any queries.

If you see something that looks ideal but aren't confident about taking the decision, give the company a call or email them with your questions. The kind of response you get will help you to take a decision on whether they are trustworthy or not.

Once you've got dates and destination sorted out, make sure you shop around. There can be wide variations of price according to which company you book with and it's often cheaper to do it online for the simple fact that you're not paying someone else to sort it out for you. At the time of booking take account of the conditions of your travel, so if you're going abroad you'll need passports and possibly visas for yourself and the children. You might also need inoculations or extra healthcare insurance; if you're thinking about car hire, you'll need to take your driving licence. Though it may seem premature, it's a good idea to make up a holiday folder and put all the relevant documentation in there. At least then it's all in one place.

Start a checklist of things you need to pack and add to it as items occur to you; this is much better than rushing around the night before trying to remember everything. I've included a sample list of my own to jog your memory. It's not exhaustive but covers the main areas and might act as a good starting point.

There are lots of items that will appear on your list which are governed by the type of holiday you're taking. If it's going to be hot and sunny, you need to consider how you're going to protect tender young skin from being frazzled. As well as sunblock, buy some soothing after-sun cream and make sure you have hats for all of you. On the other hand, if you're camping in Britain, you might be better advised to purchase yellow oilskins and sou'westers.

The holiday list

Clothes

Choose stuff which is appropriate for the conditions. If it's going to be hot, lots of T-shirts and shorts, plus a single warmer outer layer for each of you, in case it gets cold in the evening. If you're flying abroad you'll have a set of clothes to travel in which are suitable for our own climate, so you can wear them again on the way back. As well as a bucketful of socks and undies, include swimming gear if there's any danger you'll be doing any (goggles and water-wings too if the children have them).

Depending on the time of year, you'll need more substantial gear if you're staying in this country, something that will keep out the rain is not only an asset but virtually essential.

Toiletries

You should be able to get your act together on your own toiletries but don't forget to include essentials like soap, shampoo and toothpaste. Larger bottles containing liquids, like shower gel for example, are best wrapped in a separate plastic bag and packed somewhere the baggage handlers can't damage them. For the children, put in toothbrushes and a flannel or sponge (it's hard to shower without) as well as a hairbrush. Another great asset is a travel pack of baby wipes. Even if you're beyond the nappy stage, they're great for wiping sticky fingers or refreshing hot little faces during long waits in Departures. It's not much use if they're packed away in the hold, so put them in your hand luggage. While we're on this subject, these days you're not allowed anything sharp or dangerous in your hand luggage, so pack nail scissors or any other hardware that could potentially be used as a weapon in your main bag which will go in the hold.

Medical kit

I'm not talking about a portable defibrillator here, just a few basics that could save you rushing to the chemist in your resort. A bottle of headache syrup (you know the one), a few sticking plasters and a tube of Savlon will fix most day-to-day ills and remember what I said earlier about sunblock and the like: prevention is better than cure. It's miserable for the kids if *you* are feeling below par so some grown-up paracetamol is a good idea as well as something to fix a dose of the trots if you're prone to such ills.

Amusements

Story tapes or music CDs are good for in-car amusement, but according to age you might like to add colouring books, puzzle books or just plain paper for them to draw on and colour in. Also in this category I'd put their favourite soft toys. They may not be important to you but I can't imagine what a trip for us without Sadie Bear would be like; to be honest I don't want to find out. If you've got space to pack it and the destination warrants it, include a Frisbee, kite, beach-ball or cricket set – hours of fun for all the family.

Gear

Here are some additional optional items that you'll either think are really practical or very sad. A cool-bag if you anticipate hot climes but only if you can get access to a freezer for the ice-packs. A penknife, lest you should come across a horse with a particularly troublesome hoof that appears to be hindered by the presence of a stone of some kind – laugh if you must but one day you might actually need one. A universal plug (for use in sinks, etc.). Any kind of practical holiday (like camping, for example) also warrants the addition of a pair of pliers, which are the universal tool of the ham-fisted DIYer (pliers are the tool everyone uses when they don't have the right one).

Finally a Walkman or equivalent with a small pair of external speakers, so you can sooth yourself to sleep with Mantovani (again!) or put the story tapes on to amuse the kids.

When you've gone part way to getting all this organised, you can break the news to the children about where you're going. I'm always careful to make sure everything is confirmed before I do this as I can't think of any greater disappointment for them than being told they can't go on the fabulous holiday you promised them a few weeks ago. Without doubt they'll want to know all about where you're going and what you're doing so it's easy to whip up some enthusiasm and excitement. However, don't get too specific about one particular aspect of the holiday, children have a great way of becoming fixated about an enticing-sounding detail. If you're sure there's a water wonderland fun park to visit, then tell them but if you get there and find it's a large hole in the ground filled with ditch water, you're in for a bad time.

Packing

There is some law of physics which applies to holidays that I've never quite been able to grasp. It says that no matter how far in advance you book them, you will still be running round like a lunatic the night before, wishing you'd been better organised and all of this for an event which is supposed to be relaxing. There is no advice I can offer which will combat this law, all I can say is that my own strategy involves setting up a 'holiday room' at least a week in advance. As the children aren't with me all the time, I use one of their bedrooms as a repository for all things holiday and lay out on the bed the items that I currently have ready, including clothes for each of us, toiletries, books I may get a chance to read (hah!) and, of course, the vital holiday folder (not only has this got all the important documents in but I now know exactly where it is!).

I've said that the last-minute rush is unavoidable and certainly I've never been on a holiday when it hasn't happened but remember that the children don't know or understand this, all they see is a week or two of fun ahead. If, in your panic, you get ratty and short-tempered, all it will do is put a damper on the start of your holiday so be as organised as possible and even when you're not try to keep the anxiety to yourself.

The final thing to think about before you set off is that although in under a day's time you will be at your destination, you have a journey to go through first. For excited children this is a boring day that deprives them of the fun they're expecting, so lessen the pain by making sure you have plenty of snacks and drinks on board as well as something to keep them amused. A new toy, produced with a flourish at the airport, can keep a child entertained for anything up to ten minutes.

On long car journeys you can cut down on the 'Are we nearly there yet?' count by playing the story tapes or CDs I mentioned or even music appropriate to their age. Very young children will listen to the same thing again and again, though this could drive you crackers. I always think there are only so many versions of 'The wheels on the bus' that a man can join in with. I've found the local library to be a good source for this kind of thing because it's really cheap to hire, it's new material for the children and once you're back, you can return it so that you'll never need to suffer it again.

Home from home

When you do arrive at your accommodation, you'll do that strange human behaviour thing of 'socialising' yourself with your surroundings. Have you ever noticed that when you go into a hotel room or self-catering apartment for the first time you prowl around a bit, open a drawer or wardrobe, switch the light on in the bathroom and have a peek in, eat the shortbread? I've stayed hundreds of nights in hotels (when I worked in business) and the pattern was always the same. Maybe I thought that one day I'd open the bathroom door and there would be something other than a bath, sink and toilet in there. Maybe I'd find Fungus the Bogeyman scrubbing up in the bath or Catherine Zeta Jones standing at the sink flossing her teeth, who knows?

I only mention this because kids will do exactly the same (try to make sure you beat them to the shortbread) and if your accommodation is big enough (like an apartment, for example), they love it if you let them choose their own room. The placing of a favoured soft toy on their chosen bed will make it seem like home from home right away.

So, you're here, you're sorted; it's fun, fun, fun from here on in. I'm not going to tell you how to do that because if you don't know by now, you're a lost cause. The only thing I will say is that it's good to balance activities with respite. If you have a mad morning splashing around in the pool, don't then organise a ten-mile bike ride for the afternoon. I knew a couple once who took their children to the theme parks in Orlando. I'll grant you that the passes to get in are expensive so you don't want to spend just an hour there, but they went to the opposite extreme, putting their children through a 'marathon of fun' until they were absolutely exhausted. I couldn't see the point in that. To help avoid unnecessary discomfort and distress, depending on the ages of your children, 'wee breaks' can be a regular feature of the day so it's good if you can develop a sixth sense for where the loos are – sometimes you need only use your sense of smell to do this.

Also consider the need for breaks, or pit-stops as we always refer to them. This is particularly important when you are involved in a fairly active holiday, which will quickly use up the energy reserves of small children (and often their dads too). I am grateful to my older brother for the one great lesson he taught me about days out with your kids and that is you should always have drinks and snacks on hand. Now clearly this takes some organisation and forethought, which can be a bit of a pain in the arse, but it is much better than having whingey kids who are both hungry and thirsty. His innate ability to produce a pie from his pocket at a moment's notice, day or night, would be the envy of any magician.

Holidays, like all good things, have to come to an end and very often children get upset when the time comes. In fact if they can't wait to get home, you've probably got it wrong somewhere. Even if you're feeling miserable yourself, it's your duty to keep their spirits up with optimistic statements about all the great holidays to come in the future.

A fantastic idea to prolong the enjoyment, even after you've returned home, is to help the kids compile a holiday scrapbook. It's such a simple thing to do and great fun, with the added benefit that you can capture the spirit of the thing and look back fondly in years to come. As well as a selection of photographs, I try to keep a fistful of receipts from restaurants we've been to, toll bridges we've crossed, groceries we've bought, attractions we've visited, all of which go towards providing a picture of the holiday as a whole. One year the kids were highly amused by the funny breakfast cereal they had on holiday, not available in the UK, so I even cut the front off the box for them to stick in their scrapbook. It might sound daft but it is often these little things that can be so evocative of the time that you had. During the compilation process the kids even wrote their own comments alongside some of the things we put in, which of course were hilarious at the time and will doubtless provide them with hours of entertainment when they look back in years to come.

I'd shy away from saying you should keep a diary when you're away because it can become a chore, but one year my daughter did keep some occasional notes of what we'd done on a few of the days so we stuck them in the scrapbook alongside the other memorabilia as an extra reminder of what had happened.

So, I think holidays are great or at least they should be. If you think this chapter has been a bit like a military operation of careful planning, then all I can say in my defence is it's better this way than looking back with horror on what was supposed to be the best time you can have as a single dad. All the stuff you do in advance is there to make sure that nothing can spoil your fun and your kids will remember you for that. Cool or what?

9

Memories are made of this

I have a dreadful memory. Successive girlfriends over the years have had to suffer this and I've simply shrugged and told them it's a man thing. Certainly 'Whatsit' used to say that, and for that matter so did 'Hoo-jah'. In fact it's not really true at all because in reality I simply have a *selective* memory. I'm really good at remembering the things I want, it's just that they're not always the same things that others expect!

If this rings some bells with you, then I've helpfully provided here an innovative, ground-breaking solution to the problem, a single dad year-planner. There are several good reasons for me having compiled this, not least of which is the fact that I don't want my kids to think that I don't care about them. It's true that I'm unlikely to miss either of their birthdays but there are lots of other things that happen in their lives which they see as really important but I just know I would forget if I didn't write them down. Hence I've suggested the inclusion of events at school like parent's evenings, concerts or nativity plays. In addition I add on *ad-hoc* happenings as they come up so if they've said they're going to a sleep-over a week on Saturday, or to so-and-so's party, I jot it down at the time so that when I speak to them the day after I can ask how it went without being prompted.

You might think it strange but I also put my own birth-day on it. This is not because I'm likely to forget but when you get to a certain age these things come and go without you really noticing them. However, just because I've become a bit complacent about marking the anniver-sary of my birth, it's not fair if they miss out on helping you celebrate, so I always set some time aside on that day so that they can get excited on my behalf (and eat cake).

If you've suffered an acrimonious split, you might not feel too inclined to help celebrate their mum's birthday, or for that fact Mother's Day, but once again this isn't something you're doing for yourself, *you're doing it for the children*. Hopefully this will be reciprocated. I could not give a toss about Father's Day but imagine how awful it would be if the rest of the kids in class were making cards and yours said that it's not worth it because there's no cause for celebration!

Although I've provided the 'software' (i.e. the list of important events), you'll have to put in a bit of work yourself, both in sourcing suitable 'hardware' (i.e. a year-planner, etc.) and in marking it up in an appropriate fashion. A good time to do this would be at New Year when you're flush with good intentions and aside from it giving you a warm glow once it's complete, it will also last longer than any resolution you've ever made.

For me, I'd choose the wall-planner in the kitchen. This is a belting idea because *everyone* can see it and you can start to encourage the children to take responsibility for their own upcoming events as soon as they're old enough. I'm sure you don't need me to help you with your cunning colour coding but I have stuck in a few helpful hints on the list as I've thought of them. It's also worth remembering that you only have to go through this painful process once, as next year all you do is copy the dates from the current chart.

Birthdays

Don't forget to include your own, your ex's and all the other family and friends you'd normally send a card to. A good tip if you've got nieces and nephews is to put how old they will be on that day, remembering to add one when you transfer them over to next year.

Work and play

Logically, anything that's not term-time must be holiday time and as both are important in their own way, each needs marking up. Get term dates from their school and don't forget to put down the half-term breaks as well, as this is an opportunity to catch up for a few more days than usual, maybe even arrange a long weekend away.

Bank Holidays

I nearly always forget about these, which means they can be a bit uneventful because I've never got anything planned. The current list of Bank Holidays in England is as follows, bearing in mind that the specific dates can alter according to whether they might fall on a weekend (get a diary to check on the details):

- New Year Day

- Good Friday and Easter Monday (depending on when Easter falls)

- May Day and spring Bank Holiday (beginning and end of May)

- August Bank Holiday (towards the end of the month)

- Christmas holidays, Christmas Day and Boxing Day

Festivals and events

These can vary quite a bit depending on your or your kids' religion, lifestyle, etc., but don't forget to put them on your planner (or whatever system you're using).

Other

I admit that having an 'other' category is a bit of a cop-out but I couldn't think of where else to put this stuff and didn't want you to miss it:

- Mother's Day – your own mum and the children's mum (March)

- Father's Day – as above, sort of (June)

- anniversaries

Because this is a single-dad year-planner you might think it's a bit of a cheat to use it for other family birthdays and the like but there's a very good reason. Because of my selective memory syndrome I used to rely fairly heavily on my wife to write important events on the calendar and then make sure a card was despatched at the appropriate time. Now I'm single again, it's all fallen apart but I don't want my mum or sister to think that I can't cope on my own. I'd hate that.

10

In sickness and in health

This is a chapter about common sense. I say that right at the start because not only am I far from being a medical expert but because the limit to my knowledge means I can only keep my children healthy to a degree, before I need to call upon the professionals and I commend the same course of action to you. I'll say here and now that if you're worried about any aspect of your kids' health, no matter how trivial it may sound, then I urge you to seek proper advice right away, don't rely on me!

I'm sure there must be times when doctors get cheesed off by precious parents fretting over the slightest change in the look or behaviour of their children but because the risks of *not* spotting signs of illness are much greater in youngsters, they put up with all the false alarms with amazing good grace.

Prevention is better than cure

When you're concerned about the well-being of your family, you can do a lot to stop them from getting poorly. A good balanced diet is a great starting point and although children will naturally resist anything that looks healthy in favour of tasty high-fat/high-sugar alternatives, you do have to keep trying. I haven't managed to convince any child of the merit of sprouts yet but vegetables of a less 'offensive' kind are a regular part of all our meals.

'Moderation with treats' is my mantra so most of the time I'm happy to let the kids eat a reasonable amount of anything they want, as long as it's a good mixture. I once knew a guy who only ate chocolate, crisps and chips, really, that was the lot. Although he looked OK on the outside, I dread to think how his arteries were faring and the side-effect was that it made him a social misfit. It's kind of hard to find a restaurant that only serves that stuff. I blame the parents, which is why I don't want to fall into the same trap.

Exercise is equally vital in keeping us in good shape and with children there are a hundred and one ways of doing this without it being a chore. A kick about in the park or a trip to the swimming baths will hardly seem like punishment and it's as good for you as it is for them. I can't stand reading about couch-potato kids in the papers, there's just no excuse. Earlier I talked about how exercise releases endorphins and as adults makes us happier and more content; the same applies to children, with the added benefit that they sleep better and reap the rewards of that too.

While we're on the subject of sleep, it's worth remembering that this is a vital part of good health. If your kids are permanently tetchy and you can't seem to figure out why, try putting them to bed a bit earlier and see if it makes a difference. It's also essential to make sure your house is the right temperature for the children, particularly in the winter. You may not feel the cold but if they do, they'll be more prone to illness if they're constantly cold.

Physical ailments

The fundamentals of preventing illness are one thing, but as part of your duty of care you also need to guard against accidents in the home, which are by far the biggest contributor to the workload of hospital casualty departments. There's a ton of advice available from RoSPA, both in leaflet form and online, which should get you past the most obvious pitfalls, but aside from that you need to develop a sixth sense about when little fingers might get trapped in doors or hot drinks spilled onto tender skin. More than ever you need to see the world from your child's point of view.

Here is a sample of the sort of advice you can find:

- *Be aware of your child's changing abilities and learn to look at them from a safety point of view.*

- *Always keep an eye on children at play.*

- *When running a child's bath, put cold water in first then hot.*

- *A child can easily fall out of a window. Fit safety catches on all upstairs windows – restrict openings to*

100 mm (about 4 inches) and keep furniture they can climb on clear of windows.

- *A young baby can easily suffocate or choke; avoid small objects.*

- *A child can drown quickly even in only a few inches of water; stay with young children at all times when they are in the bath or in an inflatable garden pool.*

- *Place breakable ornaments (especially glass) out of reach.*

But you can go too far and never let them develop any skills for themselves. It's a question of judgement, assessing when their motor skills are sufficiently developed to be able to cope with more complex tasks.

If the worst should happen, you need to have prepared yourself to cope with the help of a basic First Aid kit. Many high street chemists stock a ready made-up family kit and you can even get a travel version which is good to keep in the car for emergencies but you can also make up your own with a bit of forethought.

Here are some items to include:

- *plasters of various sizes*

- *scissors*

- *tweezers (for removing splinters)*

- *antiseptic cream (known in our house as 'magic cream')*

- *antiseptic cleansing wipes*

- *cotton wool*

- *micropore and lint.*

The last item on the list appears because I've found on many occasions that there hasn't been a sticking plaster made which is small enough for tiny fingers and toes, so we've had to make our own 'mini-plasters' to do the job.

In addition to the First Aid items there are a number of other things in our medicine cabinet:

- *children's paracetamol suspension (now available in handy sachets too!)*

- *cough mixture*

- *cold remedy – for kids*

- *cool gel sheets – for fevered brows (note: they're not designed to reduce temperature but are soothing)*

- *hay fever syrup (good for drying up snotty noses)*

- *vapour rub or liquid (to ease congestion; I sound like an advert now)*

- *children's thermometer (some are in strip form that can be placed on the temple)*

- *rehydration salts (for after vomiting; some come in fruit flavours).*

Some of these things can be a great source of comfort if your child is feeling a little off colour; more than anything, they want to know you've *done* something for them and that can often make them feel a bit better. However, for anything other than 'a little off colour' you might need some higher level of expertise, which comes in a sliding scale of help.

At the base level you might consider calling on a trusted friend or family member who has had children themselves. Communities (remember those?) used to be stuffed full of elder stateswomen who had brought up countless children and could be relied upon to dispense good, down-to-earth advice about a range of illnesses, but sadly this is becoming a thing of the past. However, any responsible parent will give you the benefit of their experience and if they're not sure, they will probably recommend that you seek further professional help.

Under these conditions you might choose to contact NHS Direct, a 24-hour helpline staffed by qualified nurses who can give you advice there and then over the phone. There's an online version too, with lots of background information on symptoms and their possible causes, but this is only good if you've got time to browse. If you're feeling a bit more panicky, pick up the phone.

Beyond this level of care is your family GP. If you're fit and healthy yourself and have no cause to visit them, it's easy to forget that the children might need their services. Make sure you know who their doctor is and keep the number handy, not filed away so safely that you can't find the damned thing when you need it.

If I were a doctor on call, I wouldn't be enamoured at being asked to come out on a wet and windy night to someone who most likely had indigestion, but as I mentioned earlier they do seem to make a special case for children and my own experience is that nothing is too much trouble.

Almost the final course of action is the mad dash to the local hospital but make sure you know the best route (at any time of day or night) and that the one you're considering does actually have an Accident & Emergency Department. Again, children seem to get priority treatment in such places, but try to respect the fact that they are set up for real emergencies and only use it as a last resort.

Finally, and I hope you never get to this stage, if things are really dire, pick up the phone and dial 999 for an ambulance.

Emotional and mental health

So far in this chapter I've talked about physical ailments but they are only part of our overall well-being. Mental health problems are on the increase, with estimates of up to one in ten people in the developed countries suffering problems at some time in their lives.

I am indebted to my friend Professor Cary Cooper from Lancaster University for his views on how and why this has come about. He tells me it is partly due to us as individuals and our ability to cope with the pressures of life but in some measure it is also down to the lifestyles we now lead.

For adults the change in work patterns, often driven by technology which allows us to be forever accessible, is a contributory factor, along with the need to cope with the changing roles of men and women, a 'long-hours' culture, job insecurity and tougher performance management targets brought about by increases in competition. Many of us no longer live near other members of our families and there has been a steady loss of community over the past few generations which has done much to diminish our social support networks. The media too play a part in making us more self-centred and aspirational, so we have a greater tendency to look at role models and feel inadequate in ourselves.

For children, the picture is no more rosy according to Mind, the mental health charity. Research has shown that 20% of the nation's children suffer some degree of mental or emotional problems, with a third of them experiencing a continuation of the illness through to their adult lives.

Mind lists reasons for the high figures to include genetic influences, conflict, family breakdown, alco-holism, bereavement, homelessness and more; it's a grim picture and one which we don't have full control over. However, I've done what I can to detail some of the important factors in emotional problems and can only recommend that if you need further help you seek the advice of a professional.

School

Although our schooldays are often typified as being the happiest of our lives, many of us know that this is far from the case. Lack of family support, bullying and worrying about exams are some of the common factors which blight our experience. You might be able to cope with some of these problems yourself, especially if you take time to talk and listen to troubled children, but sometimes they feel unable to open up to you, so professional counselling or access to Childline or the Samaritans might help.

Relationships

You simply can't underestimate the importance of relationships with friends and family members in the life of a child. On the positive side these provide support and fulfilment but abusive relationships, which can be physical, verbal or may involve little or no communication, can be damaging to mental health. Although you can't choose friends for them, you can actively encourage liaisons which appear to make them happy, rather than their seeking to be in with the crowd.

During the teenage years it's likely the children will want to spend less time with you and more with their peers, which is a natural part of them growing away and asserting their independence, but just because they *show* their feelings towards you less, it doesn't mean that the relationship you have with them is as not important as ever in supporting their development. This outward lack of connection with you is perfectly summed up by the wise words of Mark Twain, who said 'When I was a boy of fourteen, my father was so ignorant I could hardly stand to have the old man around. But when I got to be twenty-one, I was astonished by how much he'd learned in seven years.' At some stage of their lives children have every right to believe we're fools because there are times when we are. If you see up to the age of about 12 as the 'pedestal years', when you can do no wrong, then be prepared for a plummet back to reality after that. It's a really good way of staying grounded.

Family

I was a bit worried when I first came across the research that said that the family and home environment play a vital role in the emotional well-being of children. However, the good news is that there is plenty of evidence that this can be a force for good even in homes that are no longer modelled on the 'nuclear family' (with two parents plus dependent children) – encouraging news for us single dads.

In fact the number of children living in 'nuclear' homes is on the decline and in 1996 lone parents headed 21% of families with dependent children. In most cases this is in the mother's home but about 15% of lone mothers re-marry or co-habit each year, so often the whole concept of the family can be in a state of flux.

The result of all these various changes in our society can be many-fold and I won't detail all the possible effects here. However, I have chosen a few of the higher profile or more common negative effects that can ensue for you to be aware of.

Eating disorders

Anorexics starve themselves by eating little or nothing; people with bulimia binge or stuff themselves with food and then induce vomiting. Eating disorders are more common in girls but they are on the increase in the young male population too. The average age for onset of anorexia is 15 and bulimia 18.

Concern about being overweight and low self-esteem may make youngsters prone to dieting and in extreme cases can lead to eating disorders, so encouraging children to have a more positive body image can help. Don't underestimate the task, though, with the constant exposure to messages that being thin is desirable, on television, in magazines and in the lives of role models.

Depression

The symptoms of depression can include black moods, loss of appetite, reduced energy and a lack of enthusiasm for activities normally considered enjoyable. The causes of the illness are less well-defined as it seems that the factors involved can be as many and varied as the people affected. Common reasons include family problems, concerns about the future and dysfunctional relationships, and although your GP can prescribe antidepressants, it is just as common for some form of counselling or psychotherapy to be recommended. You need to know this because sometimes the treatment can include other members of the family. That might mean you. It does no good at all to assert that this is not your problem even if it's plain that you are not the cause. Instead be supportive and nurturing, just as you would be with a more obvious physical illness.

Anxiety

Anxiety and phobias are some of the most common forms of mental illness affecting up to 2.8 million people in the UK at any one time. These ailments are linked to fear, not always of a rational kind. It could be a fear of meeting new people, of a place (school, for example) or an object, like spiders.

What often happens with anxiety is that panic attacks ensue causing a range of symptoms from hyperventilating (as if you can't get enough air in your lungs), palpitations and chest pains, sometimes so severe that the sufferer believes they are going to die; extremely unpleasant.

Tranquillisers and sleeping pills are sometimes prescribed but because of their side-effects (and the fact that they just dull the anxiety) relaxation techniques and behaviour therapy are preferable as part of a long-term solution.

Now, if that lot hasn't depressed you, I don't know what will. The important things to remember are that you need to stay aware (though not paranoid) about the types of illness that can befall your children, try (to the best of your ability) to support them through it, resist the temptation to say 'pull yourself together' and call on professional help at an early stage if you're worried.

A healthy outlook

If we're in good health, we tend to take it for granted when really we should see it as a blessing but at the other end of the scale lies hypochondria, which is bad enough if you've got it yourself but even worse if you spread it to your children. Sometimes you need to brush aside the odd aches and pains and get on with life, so don't get too fixated by every little ailment. Like most things to do with the children, if you've put a bit of thought and planning in, you'll be able to cope with the majority of eventualities.

Take prevention seriously and with luck you won't often have to call on the services of healthcare professionals, be responsible in guarding against accidents in the home and consider your sliding scale of medical support, which you can call on according to the seriousness of the malaise.

When people are unwell, there is usually some change in them, either physically or in their behaviour, so the better you know your children, the more likely you are to spot that at an early stage and put some remedy in place. There's nothing more comforting when you're under the weather than being cared for by someone who loves you.

cmon, let me entertain you

There is no longer any need whatsoever to make an effort to amuse, entertain or otherwise engage with your children thanks to the multiplicity of screen-based delectations which have replaced the need for human interaction. Maybe I'm being a bit critical, after all what's wrong with the 'Tom and Jerry Hour' on 'Boomerang' or venting your frustration on a good beat-'em-up Play-station game? The answer's 'nothing', as long as there's more to life. You can't knock the fact that the telly or PC or console will keep them amused for hours, when you need to get a bit of work done or fancy a read of the Sunday papers, but this chapter is about the times you choose to break out of all that. Interacting with kids, showing them that you're really genuinely interested in them and their happiness is the stuff of their memories and what makes you great in their eyes.

My dad was of a different generation, when this kind of involvement wasn't expected, but I can still vividly remember when he invited us to join in his occasional forays into the kitchen on some wacky project. Two I recall particularly were 'pasta' and 'potato crisps'. God alone knows what possessed him (a rather down-to-earth civil servant) to decide he was going to attempt his own homemade versions of these products, which even then were widely available in the shops, but I hope you can detect, in my writing, the affection I hold those memories in. Incidentally, both projects failed miserably, which was half the fun.

Part of being a great dad is giving them enough of these experiences to look back on in later life and although it takes some time and effort, it delivers the added bonus of becoming part of your own nostalgia in years to come. I hope that I'll hang around long enough to be able to sit in some country pub on a rainy Sunday lunchtime and hear them say, with a laugh in their voice, 'Do you remember the day we ...'

But stop! I'm getting over-sentimental. Let's get back to practicalities. You could write a whole book about things to do to keep children amused but why bother when it's been done before, loads of times. Actually, some of them are quite good if you're stuck for ideas so it's well worth a trip to the library to see what's about. A word of warning, though, they're a bit like compilation CDs. For every great track, there's an 'Agadoo' waiting round the corner that needs to be skipped past before you've even thought of 'pushing the pineapple' or 'grinding the coffee'. Nevertheless, they're worth a dip into to see what amuses you and might keep the kids happy for a while.

As single dads these days I think we're pretty lucky, simply because there is such a fantastic choice of stuff to do, from cinemas with 'surround sound', to ice-skating rinks, ten-pin bowling, family-friendly pubs and restaurants, interactive museums and fabulous theme parks. What they have in common, of course, is that they all cost money and so you can't, or shouldn't, embark on a wall-to-wall programme of these events.

Even if you can afford it, I don't recommend making every day a day-out simply because it raises children's expectations to a point which can't possibly be sustained over time. The result is that they end up spoiled. I once knew a couple who both worked full time and every weekend was jam-packed with this kind of activity; it was a strict regime of fun, like a boot camp for entertainment, with not a single moment when the kids could just slob out on the sofa. The sad fact was that as soon as they hit a Saturday morning when nothing had been planned, they lasted about a nanosecond before up went the cry of 'I'm *bored*!' The kids had never had to use their imaginations because Walt and Ronald and all their other larger-than-life commercial chums had replaced the need to.

I've done my best to seek out things that are free or cheap but I recognise that what *we* do might not suit *you*, so instead I've tried to outline ways you can draw up your own list of activities. Some families are sporty and outdoor, some more cerebral (they think a lot), others still frivolous and fun and even within your own unit you may have different types who prefer diverse amusements.

Finding the fun!

Think about some of the following things as a way of defining what will prove to be winners:

- *What do you like? What gives you enjoyment?*

- *What ages are the children?*

- *What amuses them naturally?*

- *When did you last have a great day with them? Where were you?*

- *What haven't they tried yet?*

This is a good way of starting to get an idea of what will 'wow' them.

If you once had a great day at the park, then next time you go, you take a bigger collection of outdoor stuff, like balls of various sizes, a bat, kite, Frisbee and if you've got any sense, one of those wind-up birds that flaps its wings and flies. On a good day you may even consider letting the kids have a go.

On the other hand, if your kids are 'arty and crafty', keep hold of old packaging like cardboard boxes, tinfoil, tissue paper and egg cartons. Before you know it, you will have built that rocket to the moon, or a 'diamond'-encrusted crown and necklace.

These kinds of activities may keep them amused up to about the age of 12; after that they've grown sufficiently independent not to need or want you for intensive enter-tainment. This is all the more reason to get it while you can. Soon they won't exactly be lost forever but it'll be make-up or paintballing and that's only one step away from the lifelong entertainment of pursuing the opposite sex, something they will actively discourage *you* from being involved in.

what's in it for me?

I know lots of dads who find childlike pursuits a bit, well, childish. There are probably only so many games of Junior Monopoly any of us can play, without being tempted to start robbing money from the bank every time we pass Go. There is a great benefit to this kind of intense interaction, though, in that it allows for compro-mise and gives you something to bargain with. 'OK, one more round of Buckaroo then dad's going to sit and read the paper for a bit'. Sorry, poor choice. You can never get tired of Buckaroo but I hope you see what I'm driving at.

You might even find that you enjoy this kind of thing, not because of the intrinsic reward of playing but because you get a chance to see your children 'in action', get to know their personalities and have the opportunity to 'teach' them all sorts of things, from counting and adding up through to being a good loser. My own children also find it a great bonding exercise, not so much with me but with each other as they gang up to force me into bankruptcy, or whatever else the game entails. I'm not quite sure this is such a good lesson though, as it's always me who has to be the good loser!

one to one

If you've got more than one child, you'll know they have to share, even compete, for your interest and there is nothing they like more than being made, albeit temporarily, the sole focus of your attention. For this reason it's a good idea to try to spot an activity that each child is particularly interested in, while the others find it a bore.

Try to make the opportunity to single each of them out at different times and indulge them in this shared pastime – shared, significantly, just between the two of you. These are the things that will form their super-special memories. If you have a reasonable relationship with their mum, you can arrange to pick just one of them up and spend an afternoon 'doing their thing', as long as you even it out amongst all your kids. Even if this isn't possible, you can find activities to keep the others amused (the telly, if necessary), while you foist all your attention on the chosen one.

Some bright ideas

Not all of the following activities are appropriate to all ages but most activities you undertake will have a spin-off in terms of learning. The kids will find out about planning, teamwork, aesthetics, problem-solving and more – mostly though they're just about having fun! Here's a quick list of a few things you could try. Just pick out the ones that suit you, your circumstances, your kids.

Making things: arts and crafts

This is a really big category and those books you looked at in the library will prove useful. Painting, clay modelling and papier mâché are all great fun, though it's a good idea to cover each child with one of your old T-shirts before you start messy play.

Some kids are spontaneously imaginative and will just kick off making their own zoo animals out of clay, without your help or interference. Others might need a bit of input from you to get them going, so be ready with suggestions. I usually join in and do my own thing, so we'll maybe all sit down to paint together. It's not the results that matter (in fact, if you're too good you start to look like a competitive dad) but the shared experience. Offer help when needed but not too much – I'd rather have a wobbly giraffe with my daughter's fingerprints in it than a beautifully crafted ornament for the mantelpiece.

A real winner is to pick something contemporary to make – you may remember the fuss some years ago when Blue Peter (bless them) came up with their own version of Tracey Island from Thunderbirds. The usual cheap blend of cardboard boxes, yoghurt pots and legendary sticky-backed plastic were employed, total cost around 26 pence, which had the official toy manufacturer hopping mad and weighed down with stock of the authorised version (recommended retail price £345.99).

I said elsewhere that part of the key to your children's happiness is managing their expectations, so you need to talk through with them how the final thing will look and you need to put in sufficient thought and preparation in advance to make sure you can pull it off. It's no good creating your *Lord of the Rings* landscape only to find all your Orcs falling over because you forgot to buy the double-sided Sellotape.

Food preparation

What does Birds-Eye do with all the unwanted thumbs from its fish? Most of our food is now so processed that we've produced a generation that doesn't know what it looked like when it started, or what it went through to become a heat 'n' serve ready meal (or a fish finger, for that matter). Here I go again, hankering after the good old days like I've never sat in front of the telly with a tinned Fray Bentos steak and kidney pie and micro-chips.

OK, as with all these things there's good and bad but it doesn't do the kids any harm to learn about food in its raw state, where it comes from (yes, before it gets to Tesco's) and how to turn it into something tasty and appetising. I think it's a good idea to have a go at as many things as possible, both in terms of types of food (meat, fish, vegetables, pulses, etc.) and ethnic origin (Indian, Chinese, Mexican, etc.). For pure pleasure my favourite thing is baking, simply because it's so messy and the outcome is usually sweet, so the kids can enjoy what they've made.

Like I said, it should be fun, and this is big fun, but along the way you can slip in the odd bit of knowledge on weights and measures, food hygiene or healthy eating, just don't get too wholesome.

Playing proprietary games

The Buckaroos, Operations and Mousetraps of the world are good for manual dexterity and provide an introduction to logical thinking, competitiveness, winning and losing, and cheating too. I managed to pick up a fantastic game called 'Stretch out Sam' in a charity shop for a quid. Sam is a waiter with an extendable arm. In turns you pile more dishes onto his tray, give his button a press and his arm rises vertically, section by section, until it can balance no more and the whole lot comes crashing down. It's hysterically funny, especially after a lot of lager. One day I must let the children play it ...

Next up (in age range that is) are the board games, where I have to admit I do like to cheat a lot. I do this first in favour of one child then the other, overpaying them the fines I owe, moving myself onto penalty squares if I'm doing too well (like the head of a snake in Snakes and Ladders) and generally showing myself to be a real loser. Somehow, they seem to find this highly amusing and they'll have lots of time later in life to suffer at the hands of the arrogant victor, for now let *them* be in the ascendancy.

Sports

I confess that I've always wanted to be better at sport than I am but it's an area I'm not naturally gifted in. This doesn't stop me from recognising the great benefits of sport, from the point of view of fitness, teamwork and fun. Your own children might show a preference for one single sport or even a particular genre like racket games. Encourage them in all they do and get them to try different things until they settle on their preferences, which might be no sport at all.

If they go down the route of team games, this is a great way of developing a social circle too and it's hard to match the camaraderie that can be generated by a good team spirit. Most of all I try to emphasise that old thing about the 'taking part' being what counts, over the 'winning'. It's easy to revel in glorious victory but noble to be able to keep your dignity in defeat. I also think it's great if they learn to appreciate the enjoyment of the endeavour for its own sake rather than having it spoiled by being over-competitive.

Outdoor fantasy games

Really these are just an extension of sports because I'm talking about the kind of game where you all run around like lunatics, with some made-up objective in mind. For some reason the International Olympic Committee have so far overlooked 'Cowboys and Indians', 'James Bond and the Evil Doctor of Death' or the 'Monster Round the Garden' as Olympic sports. Why is that?

Very little kids love to be growled at and chased, because from an early age they understand that when you, their dad, are involved, this is safe play, a bit scary but safe. Later in life we translate this kind of fun into white-knuckle rides at theme parks (at least I did). You can be left as breathless as if you'd run a half-marathon, with the added bonus of being in fits of giggles at the end and you'll find that all of you get the thrill of exercising your imaginations, as well as your lungs.

On a nice warm summer's day you can push the fun-ometer off the scale by adding in water. A collection of splash bombs, a hosepipe and some water pistols are hard to beat for full-on fun and should be a compulsory activity for all adults, at least once a year.

Fresh air

I'm getting really radical now. I just think that it's easy to overlook what's all around us. Getting out for a walk or a bike ride can be a great shared experience if you make it so. It's free, or at least cheap (you'll have to buy ice-creams on the way back), healthy and a great shared experience. You may be lucky enough to live near a beach or some woods. If not, there's usually a selection of local parks within striking distance and all of these things give you the chance to commune with nature before returning home to vegetate for the evening (with slightly less guilt than normal).

Government-sponsored fun

If you don't already make a habit of taking advantage of the many educational, cultural and fun things that are laid on by national government or your local council, you're missing out, especially as you are funding them through your taxes.

Libraries, art galleries, museums, theatres and art centres are just some of the places you can take the kids, for free or at least a subsidised rate, and don't be put off by the serious-sounding nature of the activities – there's a much better understanding of how to cater for families at all these places now.

It's easy to find out what's going on too, as there's bound to be a website for your area, with stuff to do. It's a good idea to get yourself on the mailing list for as many outlets as possible so you can plan ahead.

Throw a party

It's amazing how quickly children's parties change as they grow up and the jelly-and-cake phase very soon passes. It's actually much easier as they get older and want to do more adult things, like a visit to the bowling alley or to a restaurant for a meal. If you have young children, there are some unwritten rules of parties. The first thing you have to do is guarantee wall-to-wall entertainment. If you start to lose the attention of a roomful of five-year-olds, you're in big trouble. It's worth booking a local entertainer (magicians and clowns go down well), especially if you can get a personal recommendation. Have fixed start and finish times and keep it to about two hours maximum, including the time for 'tea'. Party bags are also compulsory these days and though I've long objected to the whole concept, I sometimes feel it is worth the few quid worth of crap to bribe the little buggers to leave the premises. Themed parties can be quite fun, dinosaurs, under sea or outer space work quite well but you need to put in a bit of extra effort to keep the theme consistent and if you can introduce an element of controlled mess, it'll go down a storm. We once had a kind of bran tub concept but made it more fun by filling a bucket with gunge with the plastic toys at the bottom. If you can't face the idea of having your home wrecked, you'll find loads of local church hall-type places that are happy to be hired out as long as you promise to clean up afterwards.

It's a good thing now and again to plan some fun time and as you can see, not everything has to be expensive, it just takes time and a bit of thought to decide what will make your kids happy. Nor does it always have to be the case that you go far afield to make a memory; you can turn something mundane into a bit of excitement if you make the effort. On cold days when we didn't feel much like doing anything, instead of just slobbing and watching a movie together, we created 'the video zone' by covering the floor with every cushion and pillow we could find, then we'd all snuggle down together to watch a favourite film, amply supplied with 'pop' and chocolate; much more fun.

For most of us our lives are packed with stuff to do, whether it's getting the car serviced, answering outstanding email, paying bills, mowing the lawn ... the list goes on. In fact there's always a good reason *not* to do the things that will really matter to your children and in the long run to you too. Don't feel guilty if the grass is too long because you'll find it's actually much greener on the side of the fence where you play with your children. For you the result will be the kind of afterglow you get from a session at the gym, where you come away feeling all virtuous and fit, and for the children you are putting in place the building blocks of happy childhood.

If you're still stuck for inspiration, here's my Top Ten list of old-fashioned fun things that have kept generations of kids amused and will continue to do so as long as you're committed to passing them on.

1. *Make a 'telephone' with two tin cans and a piece of string.*

2. *In autumn collect conkers and teach the kids how to play (along with all those urban myths of how to make them harder and more durable!).*

3. *Go for a walk in the woods, look and marvel at what's around you, collect leaves and pine cones. If your kids have any questions, look them up on the Internet or in the library and discover some natural history together.*

4. *Play tick or tag (or whatever you call it).*

5. *Visit a maze and lose yourselves for a couple of hours.*

6. *Go and feed the ducks.*

7. *Keep a dressing-up box of old clothes and props; join in with the kids when they use it.*

8. *Turn two old hot chocolate tins into 'stilts' by threading long string handles through holes near the top.*

9. *Go to the swings (at a quiet time so you can have a go too).*

10. *Buy a kite, then fly a kite.*

SECTION III

LESSONS

12

Teach your children well

There are lots of lessons we can impart to our children, some informal and others more closely associated with their structured education. Because my contact with my two is much less than their mum's, I sometimes have to think harder about keeping up with what is going on at school. There's a rundown in this chapter of the stages they'll most likely go through during their education but before that I've highlighted a few areas that I think are of extra importance, which, if you get the chance, you might be able to help them with.

Reading

Because they like to copy everything we do, reading to your kids from an early age gets them interested in books. Little and often is best rather than trying to keep their attention for a long spell. You might not be a natural actor but if you try to do different character voices, it helps to bring the story to life. I once witnessed a professional voice-over artist at work and later discovered that he'd done a lot of different voices on a BBC production of Noddy. Wouldn't you love to have been his kids because when he read the stories to you Mr Plod would actually sound like the 'real' Mr Plod. Even if you're not equipped with his level of expertise, making the characters larger than life and changing the sound of your voice to imply danger or mystery or any other mood will add to their enjoyment and, if you've got any soul at all, yours.

Board-books and bath-books are probably their first encounter and they'll soon learn the principle of turning the pages to find out what happens next. We had a bath-book with pictures of animals in, so every night we'd go through the routine of 'what noise does the cow make?', etc. I recall that the very last page had a picture of a turtle on it (clearly, the 'author' had a sense of humour). Exactly what noise *does* a turtle make? Given the choice, young children will often gravitate towards one particular book which you'll have to read to them over and over again. I could once recite the entire story of *Quacky-Quack-Quack* from beginning to end, absolutely word perfect; quite a party piece, I think you'll agree. Although this might get boring for *you*, the kids enjoy the familiarity especially when they know what's coming next. Friends of ours who had experienced this phenomenon said that if they stopped halfway through a sentence their toddler could fill in the next word. We tried it and it works – now that's what I call a party piece.

I used to think that it's never too early to start visiting the library until I found out that most don't open until 9 a.m. However, I am ceaselessly amazed at the ability of our nation to provide this magnificent service free of charge to all its citizens. Clearly, you get a greater choice if you go to a big library but I've always found some of the smaller local branches more appealing to the children. Firstly, the kids are not over-awed by the sheer number of books on display and, secondly, they tend to be a bit more relaxed. Often when we visit ours, we're the only ones there (apart from the librarian, obviously), so they can browse and you don't have to hush them all the time. If you hit on a rich vein of enjoyment, like the Famous Five, for example, you can have hours of fun reading to them and they'll actively seek out a new one each time you visit the library. Once the characters become familiar, they can't wait to see what happens to them in the next adventure. Keep your eyes peeled and you can also find great children's adaptations of literary classics. Our favourite is *Les Misérables* by Victor Hugo, not because I'm particularly high-brow but because it makes the story understandable for people like me who have a limited ability to follow a plot!

Sums

I'm not sure I can remember enough from my school days to be able to teach even basic maths and anyway it's probably all changed now due to some EU Directive that means we have to count in roman numerals and order our groceries by the binary system. Before you even get to the stage of formally trying to 'teach' children any maths, you can help out in a big way by getting them to understand numbers and sequences in everyday things, like counting up their buttons as you fasten them or counting out chocolate buttons as you eat them! However, and it's a big 'however', there is one fundamental item of arithmetic which should not be ignored by any responsible father: the times tables. Without this foundation in basic mathematics, you can forget the rest.

At school we used to chant the tables in order to learn them by rote and what I find quite comforting is that no one has come up with a better way since. A good record store will carry a number of CDs which have the tables set to music, so you can play them away to your heart's content on the car stereo, making sure you turn it up loud enough to mask the 'are we nearly there's?' Many of these are set to nursery rhymes but for older kids there's a much trendier version with a drum and bass accompaniment (called 'Beat It'), which helpfully includes some tracks on the basics of English too, such as when to use 'there' and 'their'.

I do make attempts to help out with maths homework now and again but so far I haven't encountered some of the mathematical horrors of my youth like Pythagoras's theorem. I'm dreading this happening partly because I can't really remember how it works but mostly because if I'm asked what earthly use it has been to me, I'll be hard put to answer. Maths anoraks amongst you will probably be reaching for pen and paper now to explain its relevance to the modern world but save yourself the pain because, quite frankly, I just don't care.

ICT

I make special reference here to ICT (information and communications technology) simply because it is so important to everyday life and will be a big part of the next generation's lives. In olden times it was known as plain boring IT (information technology) but has undergone a makeover because it now reflects not just computing but also the Internet, video and sound recording. The big word here is 'convergence' because that is what technology is doing. In future, people won't think of distinct different devices all of which perform a single function, there will be (and already has been) a coming together, perhaps on a single platform, of the technology to do lots of different things, like communicate via voice, text or email, watch video footage, access information and take pictures. I can best illustrate the difference in attitude to technology by telling you about the TV producer I knew who made a pilot programme about surfing the Internet. This was in the early days, you understand, and they thought it would make interesting watching to see someone skip merrily from one site to another, fulfilling their hunger for information and entertainment. When the show was finished and before it had been transmitted, he showed it to his 10-year-old son who yawned through the first five minutes, then turned to his father and said 'Dad, you think this is *technology* but to me it's just *life*'.

Time

One of the fun things you can teach kids is how to tell the time. It's an essential life skill and you may think about rewarding them by buying them a watch (hardly an expensive item these days). There are lots of ways of doing it and you can get a cardboard clock with hands on from any good toy shop if that's your chosen method. As well as teaching the analogue time, you should extend the lessons to cover the 24-hour clock as so many displays are now digital and in this format, but try to separate the stages out to avoid confusion. To make it more fun you can ask time-related questions like 'Is it time to go to the park yet?' or 'Is it time we had some sweets?', then make them tell you what time it is before you carry on.

The learning journey
Pre-school

Home learning can and should start from the day they are born but before you know it, they'll be integrated into the educational system. This varies according to where you are, but the English system is outlined in broad terms below. If you're looking for more information about how it works in your area, the local library will be able to point you in the right direction, or you can go online and find out from the relevant government body. The DfES (Department for Education and Skills) does a great job of this.

Lots of pre-school kids go to a nursery or playgroup of some kind and apart from giving their parents a break this a good way of getting them used to the fact that they'll be spending some time away from you. It is also a useful early introduction to other human beings their age, so they start to learn how to socialise and that, unlike at home, 'you can't always get what you want'.

With very young children it's best to keep the emphasis on fun when they're learning. That way it doesn't become a chore for either of you. At around 4 or 5 years of age children have their first school experience, sometimes being eased in gently by attending half days only at first. (I've always thought that this would be a good idea for adults at work too, I tend to find a full day just *too* tiring.) By law, class sizes are limited to 30 and many have teaching assistants in place too as it's hard to keep the attention of little ones.

Junior school

Beyond this stage (from ages 5 to 7) your child will be in Key Stage One and these early years are critical in their learning, simply because their capacity to take on new knowledge will never be greater. As well as the time they spend at school, you can turn everything into a learning experience, from a visit to the supermarket to a trip to the park. Stay aware of the risk of making life miserable by always looking like you're trying to teach them something and ask them lots of questions about their surroundings to fuel their *natural* curiosity.

In Year Two children are aged between 6 and 7 and they will face their first tests as part of Key Stage One. Some people think this is too young but at least it gets them used to the idea. The whole point of the tests is not to develop feelings of pass or fail but to give teachers a chance to work out the various strengths and weaknesses of the children in their charge so that they can adapt their methods accordingly. Because of this, part of the testing procedure involves teacher assessment on English, Maths and Science. Tests on reading, writing, spelling and maths are conducted over several days in the summer months and will last no longer than three hours in total.

Even if you don't have sufficient daily contact to know the details of what they're learning, try to take a regular interest by asking them about it and talking through the things they are covering at school. Praise them for their achievements and help them come to terms with any 'shortcomings' by telling them that everyone is good and bad at different things. If you do this, you should soon get an idea of where they might need further support from you as their education develops. It's easy for even young children to become concerned about tests so try to play down their importance and urge them to just do their best; the less fuss you make about it, the less of a big deal it will be for them. Following the tests the school will send you a report telling you how your child has fared. Make sure that you are on the mailing list, as often this kind of correspondence will go only to their mother's house.

Key Stage Two logically follows next, covering the four years between ages 7 and 11, and you won't be surprised to know that more tests are taken at the end of this period. This helps teachers in the continuing process of adapting their style, gives children a sense of achievement and provides information to the Government on how many children are achieving the expected standard, in order to inform national policies on education.

By the time children have reached this stage they will be called upon to complete homework on a regular basis and it's better if you can avoid this becoming a chore or a battleground. If they have to do homework when they're with you, make sure there is a suitable space for them to be able to work in, balance 'letting them get on with it' with being on hand to help if they get stuck and try not to make it appear that everyone else in the house is having a great time watching the telly or playing games while they're being 'punished' with work.

You might also start to investigate the many sources that can help learning be fun. As well as the library there is the local newsagent's shop where you will find magazines that are both educational and enjoyable. The Horrible Histories series is a case in point where significant facts from our past are given the kind of gory twist (including beheadings and lurid details of the plague) that have massive appeal, especially to boys of a certain age (any age, actually).

Once again, throughout this process be interested and encourage their efforts. If you have concerns about their ability or development in a particular subject, then make a point of raising it at a formal parents' evening or ring the school and make an appointment to see their teacher to chat through the various ways you may be able to help.

Secondary school
When children move to secondary school, usually at the age of 11, they will face a new challenge. This can be

a daunting prospect as they go from being the biggest, most confident kids in one school to becoming the smallest and most-likely-to-be-picked-on, virtually overnight. You can ease their journey by building their confidence at home and encouraging them to talk to you about both the good and less-good aspects of the new experience. Make sure you don't just ask about what they are learning, show interest too in the important social aspects of the move. If they've joined along with chums from their last school, then this will help to ease them in gently as they'll have someone to talk to and share experiences with right from day one, but don't be too worried if this is not the case as they tend to find new friends really quickly. Ask about who they hang around with and listen carefully to their answers. They'll always be impressed if you remember who is who and enquire as to how Josh or Catherine are getting on a few weeks down the line.

School logistics

If you're lucky enough to have the children with you for some of the week time, try to make sure they stick to a routine that works. It's a good idea if they get everything they need ready the night before so that you're not all faced with a stressful mad dash at breakfast time. The sooner you can get them to start taking some responsi-bility for this, the better – not only will it make things easier for you, it's also a really good lesson in life. Don't let them leave home without breakfast and try to ensure it's healthy and balanced. Many of the problems that teachers face with inattentive students in the early morning are down to the fact that they're hungry and/or dehydrated.

By the time they reach secondary school, children should be taking responsibility for making sure they take *everything* they need for each school day, but you can help by keeping a copy of their timetable handy and checking with them when they're preparing (the night *before*, remember) that they've got their swimming kit or sports gear.

Often, important correspondence from the school will make its way to you via the kids in their 'book bag' (which saves on postage), so get them into the habit of checking to see if they have 'post' for you, otherwise you'll miss out on trips and other essential information. With luck, you will have a civil enough relationship to be able to share this with their mother but if you're still 'at daggers drawn', contact the school office and ask that you are copied in on any significant missives.

It may be the case by this age that they have to spend some time 'home alone' at the end of the day, especially if you're working full-time, so establish some ground rules on safety, like locking doors when they come in and not answering the phone (you can set up a code, like ringing three times then calling back, if you need to get in touch with them). It's also important that they know how to contact you (on your mobile or work number), when and how to summon the emergency services and, if at all possible, have some arrangement with a neighbour who can help out at a push.

At age 11 there will be another round of tests, more comprehensive than before but once again split between written papers, lasting around five hours, in the middle of May, and teacher assessment, and as with the earlier ones you should receive a report on progress back from the school. The following years up to the age of 14 are classed as Key Stage Three, at the end of which pupils are considering their options for GCSE and/or NVQ. These qualifications are important to employers and are the foundation for 'A' levels and then on to higher education, so they'll need lots of support in their choices and course work.

Some children take GCSEs between the ages of 14 and 15 but it's more usual to wait until a year later. These two years are classed as Key Stage Four.

Hopefully that's filled in some gaps on the structure of your children's education. I've also listed here some of the more commonly used jargon of the school system.

Some school jargon

- *DfES – Department for Education and Skills*

- *GCSE – General Certificate for Secondary Education; we used to call them 'O' levels and CSEs until 1988*

- *NVQ – National Vocational Qualification; these are designed to equip people to do specific jobs and usually include some kind of regular work placement to offer hands-on experience*

- *SATs – this is the name given to the national tests and teacher assessments that happen at ages 7, 11 and 14*

- *INSET days – to the education system, these are in-service education and training days designed to update teachers' skills; to kids, they are a day off: hurray!*

- *Ofsted – Office for Standards in Education; they carry out regular inspections on all state-funded schools and produce reports which are designed to improve standards.*

The school environment is great for the formalised part of education and the National Curriculum supports learning across the key subjects that equip children for working life as well as helping to define their preferences, which may in turn govern if they'll end up as a doctor or a designer.

It's also the case that school life teaches children much more, including essential life skills around relationships and human interaction. Stay interested in this and you can have an input that complements their daytime learning, helping to shape them into confident, well-rounded, happy individuals.

⑥⑥⑥⑥

13

Life's a bitch and then you die

I already know what I'm going to write in this chapter; it's sketched out on a pad next to me and I'm not looking forward to it. I've drawn up a list of seven tough lessons in life and it doesn't make very happy reading, so all I can do is apologise to you in advance and let you know that I intend to finish on a note of optimism – stick with it. You could just skip the whole thing and move to the next chapter but that would be cheating and it would also suppose that your children will be able to go through life doing the same, never having to encounter the horrible things. It's just not very realistic.

Lesson 1: fairness

Can you remember your baby's first words? Were they by any chance 'It's just not *fair*!' Well, if not, I bet they didn't wait too long to utter this sentence and you will have an instant glib reply, which comes as standard in every 'parent's toolkit': 'Yes, but *life's* not fair', because of course it isn't. When the other team gets a winning goal in injury time, is that fair? And when your little brother gets a slightly bigger slice of birthday cake, where's the fairness in that? To redress the balance many of the laws of our land attempt to find a base in parity. Look at discrimination in the workplace; tribunal judgments are decided on how one individual is treated in comparison to another in similar circumstances. In the same arena most gripes about bosses are on the basis that they appear to have a favourite, a teacher's pet, who gets preferential treatment over others, and when you're growing up it's all too easy to see your siblings getting a better deal than you.

In some families this plainly *is* the case. You can see from the outside how the first born, or the youngest child, is able to get away with murder while others are kept on a short leash, but under most circumstances it's doubtful if it's intentional.

Inevitably, because children are different, we treat them differently but I'm resolved from now on to try and even out the spoils, the attention and the cake.

Sadly, it doesn't do much for the child concerned if you continually use your 'life's not fair' line, so where possible it's worth trying to explain why you have apparently meted out different treatment to each of them. It's also useful if you have some vague kind of ready-reckoner going on in the back of your head which says who's had what and why, because even if you're not keeping score, you can bet the kids are!

Outside the home, where you have less control (in the school playground, for example), the unfairness of life is harder to balance, so if they come home with some story of woe which involves them being done down without good reason, the best you can do is sympathise and try to explain that in the big picture things even out at least most of the time and when they don't, you just have to put up with it.

Lesson 2: they're all out to get me

Paranoia, the real kind, is a scary and well-defined medical condition but there are times when we all feel like the world is conspiring against us. By the time we reach adulthood, it's likely that we will all have fallen victim to such feelings at some time or another. It matters little whether this is real or perceived, the discomfort is equal either way and sometimes it's only when we look back that we can *objectively* see what was going on. I've been made redundant several times and can recall in the run-up to it things which went on that made me feel uncomfortable, but once you start down that track there is a dreadful spiral that can suck you below the surface and you start to believe that even your friends are against you.

In my children, I've noticed that alliances with chums seem to be made and broken on a much more regular basis on the *female* side of the family: so-and-so has always fallen out with whatsit and everyone else is divided in one camp or other by taking sides. What I love about this behaviour is that the next time you ask the question about who is talking to whom, the answer is completely different with the battle lines drawn in an entirely new configuration. Boys seem much more able to stick with the same mates for a longer time, though I am not applauding this particularly, I just recognise that much of it is brought about by their natural apathy. Basically, they can't be arsed to fall out because the effort of reconciliation is just too great.

Of course, it is hurtful when others plot against you and if you're ever faced with an 'et tu, Brute' moment, it helps if you have a Plan B. This is not easy when all your closest allies seem to have betrayed you, but a good lesson in developing self-reliance, so when the walls come tumbling down you're still left standing in the middle of the rubble, albeit a little battered and bruised.

Lesson 3: greed, avarice and other vices

I've already gone on about the kind of behaviours you might care to model for your children in the hope that they will grow up to be good citizens and happy individuals. What continues to surprise me about life is that not everyone is following that path because it seems to me that there are some people in the world who display distinctly unpleasant character traits. It's probably pointless to speculate on why that is, suffice to say that your progeny are bound to encounter individuals with a less worthy outlook on the world than you. You could stop and point out that for all their meanness of spirit, their money grabbing and selfishness it hasn't made them any happier, except that sometimes you will find it hard to prove the case, especially when they're driving around in their Lamborghini. In a situation like this we can only turn inward to ourselves and ask if we would be any more content if we behaved like them. You may resolutely hold onto the view that richness is within us and is about more than the material acquisitions we have made, but the toughness of the lesson is in the envy we all occasionally feel. Although not religious myself, I can well see the benefit of faith if it helps us come to terms with the fact that others have more than us just because they were prepared to snatch more.

Lesson 4: love's not 'always and forever'

How sad and how I wish it wasn't so. It's both danger-ous and unkind to quash the idealism of any other human being just because the experiences you've had have made you cynical, especially when it's your own kids. However, in the situation we're in it's not difficult to prove the case that people fall in and out of love, as I am making the presumption that you once felt that strongly about their mother. For all the misery that lost love causes, I remain optimistic about the whole concept of us always having the capacity to love another human being, believing that we never run out of love, that we should give it freely, though not always expect it in return, and that there are many different kinds of love (though, rather frustratingly in my opinion, only a single word for it in the English language).

Lost love doesn't mean that life's over, though it does feel shit for a while. How I wish I could adequately express that to my kids without them having to discover it for themselves. Maybe in the future someone will develop a virtual reality version so that you can experience the feeling on a temporary basis but never have to go through it in real life. You're right, now I'm just being stupid.

Lesson 5: cheats sometimes prosper

In a way we're back to 'It's just not *fair*' because it isn't but that doesn't mean it never happens. When you hear about some corporate scandal where the chief accountant has been sent down for embezzling millions from the company's coffers, you can't help wondering if there are others who are doing likewise and getting away with it. It's like unsolved crime: we know it exists, so someone somewhere is getting off scot-free.

All of this heightens the temptation to indulge in a bit of well-timed duplicity to further our own ends but in the final analysis we all have to be able to live with ourselves and I'm never proud if I've won out because of foul means rather than fair.

The other damnable thing about cheating is that it's not clear-cut. Look at the world of football; a dreadful foul committed by an opposition player is met with derision but the same offence perpetrated by a team member in *our* colours is regarded as nothing more than a 'strong and robust challenge'. Similarly, we pass off other minor misdemeanours in front of our kids with euphemisms like 'a little white lie'; maybe it's just part of survival.

Lesson 6: the love of money is the root of all evil

Some of the n'er-do-wells mentioned above will go to any lengths to increase their wealth, and money does have a way of coming between people. Special mention here goes to con-men (why always men, it's neither politically correct, nor I suspect strictly accurate). As a kid, I went to a fairground with my brother and we were conned out of some of our pocket money by a slippery stall holder, only realising the sting too long after the event to do anything about it (I should point out that he was considerably bigger than us too, so I wouldn't have rated our chances of a fair hearing). I felt really done down, and the fact that I can recall the details even now says something about the lasting effect it had on me. In consumer advice circles the current cliché 'if it looks too good to be true, it probably is' is not a bad lesson to teach, I think.

Money can come between the best of friends too and I daresay you may be able to think of a case where the same has been true of a couple of married people of your acquaintance. Sometimes, though not always, this has nothing to do with the amount of money involved but the principle behind it. Of course, on other occasions you might say 'Bugger the principle, show me the money'.

Even without the assistance of our former partners we seem to be increasingly ready and able to get ourselves into money difficulties. Surely if the credit card company I use really knew how fragile my income was month to month, they wouldn't continue to offer me such large sums to spend, or maybe they would. After all they can always take away my house, probably my kids too, if I bothered to read the small print.

Lesson 7: friends can let you down

It may appear from the lessons above and the threads running through the rest of the text that I try to put more emphasis on my relationships than on my relative wealth. That's true, but the problem with any investment (including emotional ones) is that they can go down as well as up and there's nothing more upsetting than a friendship gone wrong. Sometimes I think it's my own fault that I expect too much from other people, but I have made stringent efforts over recent years to try to be more forgiving and endeavour not to expect that I'll get in return what I choose to give out. Sorry, that sounds like I'm making all the effort here, which is not true, I have very generous friends who I can call on in an instant if I'm in crisis. In that way at least I am blessed.

Still, there are times when I see the kids making all the effort and not getting much back and I always feel sorry that they have to learn this lesson the hard way.

I know all this has been rather depressing stuff and I did promise a note of optimism at the end, so here it is: there are two states which govern all our lives, there are the things that happen to us and the way we perceive them. I believe there's little we can do to alter the former but our *attitude* is very much within our gift. Our attitudes to life are mainly in our heads. In fact, that's where I live most of my life because it's warm and cosy in there and I find it easy to be happy because of that!

I am far from being the least cynical person on the planet, but I do try to check myself from time to time, especially when faced with the innocence of youth. For all of us, we're simply trying to strike the right balance between the kind of naivety that draws us into making the same mistakes over and over, versus the hard-bitten world-weary versions of ourselves that can make life an even bigger misery.

Come on, it's not so bad.

14

Sex and drugs and rock and roll

This chapter title is a kind of generic shorthand for all the adult things which babies are born knowing nothing about (lucky things). I, along with many people my age, lament the passing of what we see as an age of innocence, where children were allowed to spend a respectable amount of their lives in childhood, before they became exposed to the vices of grown-ups. I can't change the way things are now, so better just get on with it and find the optimum way of dealing with the issues so that the children are well equipped to cope with what is to come.

Each of us has our own morality, a sense of what is acceptable and what isn't. You may not agree with where I set my personal boundaries but I hope that the principles I apply will ring true for you and you can adapt what's here to suit your personality. Let's start with sex, I can't think of anything better.

Honesty is the best policy

Around about the age I was discovering about sex, a lot of rumour and misinformation was abroad among me and my mates. I was lucky in many ways that our school was enlightened enough to get a specialist in sex education to come and tell us where babies came from, but this didn't stop the gossip, not all of which was helpful. For a good few weeks, all the boys in my class believed that when a girl had a period each month she bled from her breasts! It was only later that we discovered the truth – it was her belly-button.

In the same way I've never quite got my head round that thing they used to tell kids about the stork bringing the new baby or that it was found under a gooseberry bush. Were they really so ashamed of the fact that it was a result of their shagging and if so what kind of message does that send to kids about the beautiful and poetic coupling of two people when they become as one or, for that matter, the amount of fun you can have when you're shagging?

You may assume by all this that I believe you should tell kids the truth, no matter how early they ask the question. If we believe that honesty is the best policy and then we spend ages instructing our children not to tell lies, why would we choose to be deceitful about such important issues? If I was looking at it through child-like eyes, I may be drawn to the conclusion that there was something sinister about adult life, which is why they try to hide it from you all the time.

Natural curiosity has an endearing way of manifesting itself in the 'why' phase of development: 'Dad, why is the sky blue, why do cows go moo, why is your willy that shape?' There is no difference in the *weight* of these questions, they are all equally puzzling to inquiring minds, they don't sit and think 'Ha, I'll lull him into a false sense of security with the sky and cow questions then, when his guard is down, I'll hit him with his willy'.

If you change the weight of the answer, giving full scientific evidence to support one and skirting around another, you will be sussed out in an instant. To be perfectly honest, I'd rather be in a position to tell the truth pre-puberty than to have to explain the functions to an adolescent who has already started to function, so to speak. The same rules on honesty apply for me across the spectrum of adult issues, mostly when I'm asked about them, but sometimes more proactively, like if there's a current news story that prompts me, e.g. a rock star dying of a drugs overdose.

The following notes are not an instruction manual. You don't have to set time aside on a Saturday morning to have 'lessons in adulthood' but you might think about imparting some of this information at the appropriate time over a number of years of the children's development.

Sex, making babies and having fun

At a base level of biology, children need to know how they were made and when the time comes, how they will make one of their own. If it doesn't come up in conversation at some point, I'd be amazed but you can still find the right time to chat through it with them if you feel you need to. Sex education in schools is much better now than it used to be, so before the age when they can indulge in such activity, they will at least know about its consequences.

Finding the right terms to use is sometimes difficult with children. There's a hilarious Willy Russell play called 'Breezeblock Park' which illustrates this point really well. The social climbing mother has taught her son the correct anatomical names like 'penis' and 'vagina' but secretly the down-to-earth dad has introduced slang versions like 'knob'. Thinking this is something the boy has picked up in the school playground, the mother is appalled but it is precisely because the language of the bike sheds is more earthy and honest that the dad has intervened, to stop his son being laughed at. There is probably some kind of halfway house for most of us. All families have their own pet names for their 'bits', some of them universal, others idiosyncratic, but whatever you call your tackle among yourselves, this is the best way of imparting information about sex; it just makes it all the more normal and acceptable.

I think it's a shame that sex education seems to focus on the functional rather than the fun. It's pointless to suppose that developing adolescents won't find out about this for themselves when the first stirrings of sexual feelings start to occur, so why not let them know that along with the making babies stuff, adults indulge in 'nudey-prod games' for the sheer enjoyment of it? This is not a licence for promiscuity if it's handled properly and balanced with the reality of what casual sex can result in.

Having established that it can lead to procreation it's also fair to explain that not all pregnancies are welcomed, particularly when the participants are very young and for this reason it carries with it both a sense of risk and a need for responsibility. Tell them about contraception and, in particular, condoms. While we're on the subject, it's a small leap to introduce the topic of sexually transmitted diseases. It's for you to judge, depending on the age and maturity of your children, how much detail you go into on these subjects. Suffice to say you are presenting the case both for and against sexual activity, so that they know some decisions have to be taken when the time comes about its efficacy.

Lust versus love

It takes a long time, well beyond the relentless pumping of post-pubescent hormones, for us to understand the real difference between our sexual encounters, based on whether we were fulfilling a bodily function or transmitting our deep affection to another human being in the most intimate way we know.

Most adults have had sex without love. For some maybe that's the only sex they've had and we'd all like to protect our children from feelings of being used. Sadly, it's a lesson they're probably going to have to learn the hard way. That doesn't mean you can't warn them about it in advance. If you only ever talk about sex in an oblique way, you will never be able to make them understand its power for good in a loving relationship. Some reference to your own past is a good way of explaining about alliances that have worked and ones that haven't but you don't have to give chapter and verse, just an overview that helps to explain the point you're making about love.

More than anything I think it's right to try to get them to understand that sex under any circumstances means *something.* It's still a commonly held view that when women have sex, they're giving something away but I think that the same can apply to blokes as well. Hey!, maybe we're more sensitive than they think.

Substance abuse

I could talk only about illegal drugs here but booze and fags are just as bad, sometimes the more so because we tend to classify them as safer. Put the consequences, both long and short term, to one side for a minute and I guess we'd all be taking drugs. I think it's fair to suppose that people who indulge in any of these things find it highly pleasurable, otherwise why would they bother? But the key issue here that stops me from 'scoring' on behalf of my kids is that there *are* consequences, many of which are dire, some fatal, so recognising the buzz that people get doesn't make me pro-drugs, it makes me a realist.

I'm not trying to be right-on and trendy here so that my kids will think me cool, I'm attempting instead to apply the same values that I have in other aspects of their upbringing to a more controversial subject. If you try not to lie to them, so that they can see how important honesty is, how disillusioned will they be if at some point they're tempted to try something which you've told them is the root of all evil yet turns out to be a source of some temporary feeling of extreme well-being? Like most 'adult' pleasures, drugs don't come without some major potential difficulties but ignoring the buzz is naive.

Rock and roll

Having stolen this chapter's title from an Ian Dury song, I am compelled to follow it through and talk about rock and roll, though there's not a lot to say, really.

If we're examining the subject of popular music as a whole, there is only one Golden Rule: you're not allowed to like what your children do. Even if all the best songs in the charts have been nicked from our era and turned into watered-down cover versions with soft-porn videos to boost sales, you still have to concede that the music of today is rubbish. I don't care if you disagree, just dig out your 'dad contract' and you'll find in subsection 12, paragraph 3, near the end of page 8: 'It is the Golden Rule of fatherhood that you must detest the music of your children; furthermore at regular intervals you must issue statements such as "What's this din?", "There's no tune or proper words in this" and "Turn that bloody thing down, will you?", followed by an anecdote about when you went to Live Aid in 1985, which may as well have been *1895*, as far as your kids are bothered.'

Things have changed radically in the marketing of music and nowadays (a word only used by old gits like me) kids no longer wait to the respectable age of 14 or 15 before dipping into the musical equivalent of sweet cider – they're at it from about 8. Thank you so much

Britney. Resistance is futile, it's much better to concentrate your efforts on convincing them how cool a personal stereo looks. Whether it's CD, MiniDisc or MP3, the great benefit is that you won't be subjected to the drivel that they're listening to. If you're so inclined, the arena of music is a great place to wind them up in, either by talking in a language far removed from theirs: 'Oh, that sounds nice, is it in the hit parade?', or by getting the names of their favourite artists wrong on a consistent basis: 'Oh, who's this, is it DJ Master-Flash-Bang-Wallop-In-Da-House?' They hate it even more when you try to talk 'street' with them.

To be momentarily serious, as far as all music goes, whether it's my taste or not, I try to encourage the kids to see it live, simply because it's authentic that way. It might be authentic loud crap as far as you can hear but at least it's not fake.

Inevitably, this will mean that you will have to accompany them to some excruciating gig or another and be subjected to a couple of hours of agony but you won't be alone. The audience will be split down the middle between screaming girls aged 8 to 12 and their mums – hmmm ... maybe not such a bad idea after all. At a tribute band gig I was once the only father, it really made me rather proud. Actually, there was one other bloke there, sat at the back on his own, coat over his knee, scary or what?

Bad people

Rapists, murderers and paedophiles aren't hanging around on every street corner but let's not pretend (to ourselves or our children) that there aren't individuals with malevolent intent in the world. Exercise some common sense on this subject or you can risk making your children fearful of everything. Statistics don't mean much if you've been a victim but it is rare and you have to be tremendously unlucky to fall prey to serious crime.

At a much lower level there are other dangers to guard against, like violence. I've always thought that boys are born with an innate sixth sense that tells them when trouble is afoot. I personally have never witnessed a spontaneous and unexpected outbreak of violence. If you're in a pub and something 'kicks off', you could always see it coming, there's something in the atmosphere; I bet the same is true in the playground. My basic rule has always been that if you don't want to get hurt, get out. This might not sound terribly brave but that's because I'm not and furthermore I sense that the risks are getting greater because for every bully who just wants to indulge in a bit of fisticuffs, there's another nutter with a knife. OK, in mathematical terms this is unlikely but I don't really want to hang around to test the theory. I'm not sure what you can usefully teach your children on this subject, maybe just to stay aware of what is going on around them and try to avoid doing things that will escalate a volatile situation.

Swearing

It's not big and it's not f***ing clever but profanity is part of society. I actually think it's rather endearing when they come out with something they've heard and don't know what it means. I once did the very same thing at the Sunday lunch table when I was about five years old. Somehow I managed to slip the 'C' word into the conversation (the most profane of all, by popular opinion) and after a moment's stunned silence and some suppressed mirth from my parents, they just moved the subject on. I guess it would have been pointless to wash my mouth out with soap and water, as I didn't know what I'd said.

Most of us have 'A' list and 'B' list swear words. I won't detail the former – you can do that for yourselves – but 'bugger', 'shit' and 'bloody' all come into the second category. I do *try* not to use any at all but now and again one slips out and I don't consider it to be the end of the world. If the children swear, I don't let it pass unnoticed but equally I think that there are worse things and I believe what they really need to know is that it's all about context, so choosing when and where you use profanity is more important than not using it at all.

Once they hit the playground of 'big school', usually at age 11, you can be sure they'll have heard everything you have and more, within the space of about 15 minutes, so pretending that such vulgarity doesn't exist is pointless. Without being all sniffy about it, people who swear relentlessly are showing rather a lack of imagination in their use of the language. I've even heard the 'F' word used in the middle of another and once you've reached that level of frequency, it becomes meaningless, anyway. I always wonder what people like that say when they're *really* angry, surely there's nothing left.

Nudity and body changes

I'm not sure where our attitudes to nudity come from. I can't remember us all strolling round the family home in the buff when I was growing up but I'm not at all worried about my own children seeing me naked, except for the shock it might cause them! They too have different attitudes, with one parading quite openly and the other being much more shy. I really don't know how this comes about because I can never recall treating them any differently as they were growing up.

However, no matter what their current attitudes are, these may change as their bodies start to. Although I loathe the current political correctness that can see you arrested for photographing your own baby in the bath, I do understand the necessity for child protection. At the same time I believe there is a lack of appropriateness if you don't encourage a certain degree of modesty once they start to become adults. I am trusting that like a lot of things this will come about naturally, without the need for discussion, but at the same time I hope that our relationship will continue to be sufficiently open for them to ask questions about what is happening to them, if they feel the need to. As with the issue of sex education, I'm less bothered by the practical aspects and more concerned to help them through the emotional problems. I don't recall being worried in any way about the appearance of hair on my body or my voice becoming lower, except that I wanted it to all happen much more quickly. The only thing that ever concerned me was the thought of my balls dropping; would they make a clanging sound when it happened? The reality was that this was a load of bollocks (literally), it must have happened overnight because I never really noticed.

For dads, periods are a bit of a tricky arena because we can never really empathise very well with how it must feel. I have more than a vague second-hand notion that it's not the pleasantest time of the month, though I can recall that the line fed to girls of my age was that 'When you do start, you may feel a little discomfort and might possibly get a mild tummy-ache'. I think the opposite is much more common with massive mood swings and tears for seemingly no reason and stomach ache that would floor a buffalo. As with childbirth, it's a good job Mother Nature visited periods upon her own sex, otherwise we'd be taking to our beds for one week in every four.

Still, if we can't be properly *empathetic*, a bit of well-timed *sympathy* doesn't go amiss and if you're wise, you'll realise that the volatile moods are part of the monthly cycle and try to accommodate them without criticism. I'm told by women friends that even though they know the reason for their unreasonableness, they can't do anything to control it.

During my own development we were told all about hormones, which were described as 'chemical messengers'. That means as little to me now as it did then, except that I do know that boys and girls both have them in abundance and the only messages they seem to carry are 'I hate you!' and 'It's not fair!' I must try to resist the urge to patronise them and say, 'Don't worry, it's just your hormones', as I suspect this will simply up the ante.

So much for some of the physical changes. They are small fry compared to the emotional fallout of yearnings, crushes and permanent 'stiffies'. I'm sure it would be much better if you started to develop all these things from the moment you were born so that their impact was evened out a bit, but such feelings seem to me to be a little like buses: you spend ages waiting around while nothing happens, then they all come at once. When it comes to boyfriends/girlfriends, it can be very confusing deciding which one to go out with and inevitably they sometimes choose badly and end up getting hurt. Sometimes you can see when your offspring have chosen a bad 'un but there's nothing you can do about it. Worse still, when the wheels fall off, you have to bite your tongue and resist the urge to say 'I never thought he/she was right for you'.

Growing up

I sometimes look at my children and wish they weren't growing up so quickly. I wish they could retain the innocence they were born with but you have to be realistic and with all these issues I'd much rather have some influence over their views, attitudes and learning than leave it to chance. If you're going to let someone else 'educate' them about adulthood, you're taking a risk as you can never be sure who that person might be. Just as with illness, prevention is better than cure, so with adult stuff the knowledge that helps you avoid the pitfalls might be invaluable. As far as I can see, prevention is also better than pregnancy, rehab or disastrous taste in music.

This adult stuff can seem a bit grim but it's going to happen, so we have to face it. Like all other phases of our children's development, the best possible thing we can do is equip them with the skills and knowledge to help them through.

BEHAVIOUR

15

Dictatorship or democracy?

Rules are made to be broken, at least I think that's right. One of our most enduring qualities as human beings is to push the boundaries, right to the limit sometimes; occasionally, we go beyond that. Let's suppose just for a minute that the earth really is flat and that you and a group of mates set off to find out where it ends. When you got to about a mile from the edge, do you think someone would say 'It looks to me fellas like the edge is about a mile from here, let's go home and tell everyone', nope, someone would want to get a bit closer, then closer still until you were right at the edge of the planet, then eventually, when someone fell off, you'd know where the boundary was.

This rule applies in exactly the same way in our relationships. Remember when you were married? Just fancy if you said you were going out with the lads to the pub one night, if she kissed you fondly on the cheek and told you to enjoy yourself, not worry what time you were back or how drunk you were, the greatest chance is you'd try the same tack the next night. In fact, it's only because you came in a bit tipsy one night and she was standing there metaphorically in curlers, face-pack and armed with a rolling pin that you knew you'd over-stepped the mark. I admit this is a harsh way to learn the lesson but you learned it nonetheless.

Children are exactly the same – they need to know where the limits are and very often they can only find them by going beyond them. There are more suggestions on how to deal with this in Chapter 16 but before that let's look at how you set the boundaries, which rules are worth sticking to and who has the final say over what is accept-able and what isn't. We'll also take a peek at rule-bending, which is a necessary part of the whole process.

There are some households, of course, where it looks like there are no rules. You've probably been in one at some time: the kids run riot; do as they please; refuse to action the smallest of requests; and are generally anarchic. In such circumstances I've never thought they looked happy and I think part of the reason kids fight with one another, behave badly or make a din is because they just want attention. If you bear in mind that much of what we do as parents is in the interests of preparing our offspring for the outside world, then they may as well learn about rules right here at home. If they don't, just as with sex or drugs, someone out there in the real world will soon teach them and you can have no influence over how that happens. Suffice to say it will be a much more painful experience if they've never had to play by the book before.

There are different levels of rules you can put in place for the smooth running of your own household, so here are a couple of extremes to be thinking about.

Dictatorship: the case for and against

In this scenario you are the almighty despot who sets the guidelines by which everyone must live. What's great about it is that you don't have to model any exemplary behaviours yourself. In fact the adage is 'Do as I say not as I do'. Even better, you are free to change the rules whenever you want to suit yourself and need never justify why you do this. Mainly the guidelines are in place for your own benefit, and failure to comply results in the most dire consequences for the perpetrator – let's opt for that then, shall we? Well, I'm afraid to say it does have its downside. You can expect that there will be a continual process of plotting against you, which eventually will result in a devious conspiracy sparking a *coup d'état* of frightening proportions. All this is a rather flowery way of describing what the rest of us call teenage rebellion. This is not to say that you can future-proof yourself against the grunts and door-slamming of this least-endearing stage of development but we can all think of examples of repressed regimes where the parents have suffered many-fold more in comparison to the norm, once the kids have reached the age of rebellion.

The other difficulty of suppressing kids' natural desires to exercise their rights at home is that they may choose to do it outside, which risks turning them into a bully or a Billy (of the No-Mates variety). They need an outlet for their individuality so better to explore and learn about it behind closed doors and the 'safe' environment of the home before they take it into the school playground.

Democracy: the case for and against

In the West we tend to think of democracy as a Good Thing, allowing all members of society to have an equal say in how affairs are run, indeed Emmeline Pankhurst would be proud to see that what she started has resulted in a belief that all human beings are equal within a democratic state; there are limits, though.

'We really think that Tarquin and Jocasta should have a say in everything we do as a family'. Yes, you could just punch them, couldn't you (the parents that is, not the kids ... don't know, though)? If you can raise a child through to adulthood without them ever uttering the words 'It's just not *fair*!' you should be locked up for the good of society as a whole. Living in an idealistic democratic state where everyone gets a vote on everything reduces life to a lowest common denominator where no one is ever truly happy because you're all so busy compromising on what you want for the sake of everyone else. You may think in some misguided way that this teaches children the value of going with the majority but such a level of over-consideration for others is likely to make them end up as a doormat.

These two states are at opposite extremes and the sensible way forward is to choose somewhere on the continuum between them, but where exactly, and does it vary according to circumstance? It's for you to decide what the rules are and how to apply them, and in all honesty these things tend to just evolve over time without much thought or planning going into them; we just act in a certain way. I don't say that you need to move this thinking onto a conscious level and draw up a chart that says what is and isn't acceptable but I do believe it's worthwhile considering if you've got the balance right, both for you and for the kids. While you're doing this, it might be worth thinking about what it is that makes us as individuals behave in a certain way, so here are some factors that I think affect the kind of regime we're likely to put in place.

Heredity

First, we will be heavily influenced by our own upbringing. That's not to say we'll copy it, in fact sometimes just the opposite. If your parents were very strict, you'll either see this as a role model for child-rearing or will kick against it because it was something you didn't enjoy when you were growing up. Sometimes that teenage rebellion thing, where we go against everything our parents say and do, has a lasting effect, so if your childhood was blighted by rules and regulations, it may well be that you're more lax with your own kids so they don't have to suffer what you did. I once saw a satirical cartoon that portrayed this by showing the grandparents and grandchildren as 'spaced-out' hippies and the 'in-between' parents as buttoned-up conservatives, illustrating that as each successive generation rebels against the last, what goes around eventually comes around.

Lives and times

I looked at length in Chapter 5 at the whole issue of living in 'our times' rather than a past era so it's inevitable that peer-group influence will have some sway here too. The difficulty when you're a single dad is that you don't often get the chance to see other single dads in action so you can only guess at how they're coping. However, one sure way of finding out what it's like in other households is to listen to the feedback you get from your children about what their mates' lives are like. As well as telling you who's got the trendiest, newest trainers, they'll also tell you things like 'Nick's not allowed to talk on a Saturday afternoon as his dad watches the racing, gets drunk and farts all afternoon and he doesn't like to be interrupted'. You can also feel pretty smug about being a better father than him (as opposed to being a better farter than him).

Self-esteem

How you feel about yourself has a huge impact on the way you behave towards others and that includes children (your children) as well as adults. If your self-esteem is at an all-time low, the last thing you want to do is feel worse by being a bad father and the easiest way out of that scenario is to treat the kids all the time because then they won't give you any grief. Sadly though, as discussed earlier, this isn't a sustainable strategy as just in the example of finding the edges of the flat earth, kids will keep pushing for more and more until you get to the point when you can't deliver. You gave in on the quad bike but, really, a private Lear jet is a step too far.

Sometimes, when your children shout and scream about how unfair you're being, or worse still sulk because you won't give them what they want, you have to take it on the chin and do everything you can to convince yourself that it's all in your best interests in the long run.

As well as your own personality traits, you have to take account of the character of the children. If they're shy and compliant, they'll do what you say without question but most kids have a bit of the devil about them and to suppress it too much is to deprive them of the right for self-expression. Ultimately that will influence them in adult life so it's a tricky balance you're trying to achieve. It's also ridiculous to expect that you have the influence over what the rules are, as in many cases you won't be the primary carer. If the children spend the majority of their time with mum, it's fairly obvious that they'll be more used to her regime than yours. I'm not a great believer in trying to replicate that exactly and children certainly have an innate ability to adapt to whatever household they're in at any one time, but it's not particularly healthy for them if there is too much contrast, e.g. very strict in one home and 'anything goes' in the other.

Some of the influencing factors are less fixed than others and it may be that for some time feelings of guilt or being under stress will go some way to govern what you find acceptable. I for one was certainly more short-tempered around the time of the relationship breakdown, so I'm certain, looking back, that the rules were a bit stricter then. However, over time this evens out and you reach some kind of status quo where everyone understands where the boundaries lie even if they decide not to stick to them.

Once you've considered these things and come to a view of how relaxed or aggressive your own regime should be, you need to come up with a framework for implementation. How do you assess what is fair and what is right? Reading lots of worthy books on parenting might help you but personally I prefer to rely on instinct mixed with a good dose of common sense. You don't have to be a genius to work out when bedtime should be and if you're feeling laid-back and lean towards democracy you'll take into account both the children's views and your own before you decide what time to kick them upstairs to 'beddy-byes'.

Whatever value system you have, it will provide a good benchmark for rule-setting. If politeness is on your list, you simply have to decide what this looks like in practice, bearing in mind we're living in the 21st century, not the 19th. Check back on your other values and apply the same criteria to decide on what is and isn't acceptable.

This can all start to sound a bit too planned, whereas in reality we react in a much more spontaneous way to what's going on around us. The benefit of putting a bit of thought into it ahead of time is that you're much more likely to be consistent in the way you apply the rules. Now, kids can put up with a lot, especially when it comes to adapting to their circumstances and who is in charge of them but what they're not very good at is inconsistency. If one day it's OK to talk to you in a bit of a cheeky way, but the next day not, they're bound to get confused. They're very good at picking up moods and understanding context so behind closed doors my two will happily refer to me as a 'fat baldy git' (which of course I'm not) but know that in certain company (not all) it would be less acceptable. In our flat-earth analogy we talked about trying to find the edge, the boundary, if you like. What happens when you're inconsistent is that one day the kids stray too far, believing the edge to be further away than it is, then they simply fall off and it hurts like hell.

How strict you decide to be will also be governed by your time and patience. If you don't have very long with the children, it seems an awful waste to spend it arguing and if they are in a particularly irritating mood, you should be able to hold your own temper in the knowledge that they'll soon be going back to mum. On the other hand, if you're the one who's being moody, you sometimes need to snap yourself out of it because the converse applies, they will value the time you spend together, so it's not fair to make them unhappy by being snappy. If we've ever had a bad-tempered day (on either side), I've always been full of regret when I've taken them back to Mum because I've usually been able to see how I could have handled it better and defused the situation rather than escalate it.

Here are a few final thoughts on rules and regimes. If you decide *consciously* not to have any, then you're not doing your parental duty; if, on the other hand, you just *can't be bothered*, because it only causes arguments and you have enough conflict in your life, your dereliction of duty is just as great.

With two children they can happily wind each other up until the cows come home and then argue about whose cow is the better looking. Sometimes you have to let them get on with this, as it's an important part of learning to compromise (or understanding that he who punches hardest usually gets his own way) but equally there are occasions when a well-timed intervention will prevent the situation escalating.

Sorting out disputes between children is like trying to bring about world peace; it's difficult and exhausting but in the end much more likely to succeed through negotiated settlement than resorting to violence and counterattack. Try whenever you can to balance the outcome between the warring factions so they take it in turns to 'win'. If you always find in favour of one party over the other, the disputes can just escalate. Remember what I said earlier about consistency and try to apply similar rules in like situations and try also to understand that the right to appeal is a good thing sometimes. If you're arguing about bedtime and give ground by 15 minutes, it doesn't mean the whole 'regime' will tumble but it will help to teach about compromise.

Most important of all is to actually have some rules in the first place, then at least you know when the boundary has been well and truly breached. One final thing when it comes to keeping order: good luck, believe me, you're going to need it!

16

Don't make me angry

Discipline can be very tricky because you're trying to balance good manners and acceptable behaviours with allowing your offspring the freedom to express themselves. It's worth having a good long think about how you're going to do this and making some resolutions. This way you'll avoid reacting to every situation according to how you personally are feeling at the time.

I confess that this was an area I really worried about at first, partly because I knew that what was allowable at Mum's would be different to at mine – I was afraid the children would become confused. That was until a good friend (female, intuitive, you see), said 'Did you ever ask your dad for something and if he said "No" you went and tried the same thing with your mum?' I admitted I had and she pointed out that children are brilliant at being able to understand that they might get a different reaction from each of you, and consequently they can play both of you, *irrespective* of whether or not you live under the same roof.

So, the good news is that you *can* set your own rules on what is and isn't acceptable. My experience is that single dads tend, in general, to have a more lax attitude to discipline, partly because under most circumstances we see less of the children and don't want to be warring with them all the time and partly because they have less time to wind us up!

However, as I've said, I would caution against a regime that is *fundamentally* different to mum's – they do need to understand some core principles of acceptable behaviour and I'm assuming that you and your ex had a common view of this at some stage in your past. Being too laid-back will only result in your being accused of trying to 'buy' their favour ('Well, Dad lets us stay up late ...') and you can guarantee that, on the basis of this, you'll be held solely accountable for them being caught shoplifting when they're 14.

I think that if you do keep the whole discipline within boundaries that are more or less acceptable to all, then it's fair to expect your ex not to interfere with your regime, as long as you don't interfere with hers. Only you can decide what's OK and what's not but have a look at the story that follows and think about how you might have reacted and why.

crime and punishment

Sam, aged 7, was having tea in Auntie Anne's kitchen. Dad poured him a beaker of milk and set it down on the table, with the words 'Don't knock that over, Sam' but moments later he did just that and spontaneously burst into tears.

Auntie Anne (herself a mum of many years' experience) swooped with a cloth in one hand and using her spare arm to cradle and soothe Sam. It was all over in seconds with the crisis averted. Before you start criticising the heavy-handed naffness of this 'no good crying over spilt milk' story, I have to tell you that it's absolutely true. More than this, it's taught me lots of useful lessons about discipline.

I say this, because my reaction would have been to shout, especially if I'd just said 'Milk-alert – be careful! – Earth-to-Sam, come in, over, I'm putting this down here – don't spill it'. Auntie Anne's reaction to the situation made me believe that there may be a different way.

Important lessons
Kids are clumsy
The truth of it is, they're learning their skills of coordination bit by bit, their hands are smaller, their muscles weaker. They'll be like this up to a certain age (my brother claims it's about 21), so learn to live with it. When they're tiny, you can mitigate against spillages with bibs and sealed beakers but eventually 'Tommy Tippee' will have to give way to a pint glass, so give them the chance to learn, safe in the knowledge that some milk will get spilt.

Accidents will happen
It's not just kids who do this kind of thing, remember the last time you did? So, whose fault was that then? Suddenly the whole idea of shouting about it becomes

rather pointless. You may as well save the energy for the clearing-up operation.

A sense of proportion

No one died did they? An easily moppable liquid on a lino floor and Formica table (that's how classy we are in my house). Kids teach you a lot about the pointlessness of coveting your worldly goods too much. As babies and toddlers, they have no sense of the quality of your pale beige carpet, or Bose speaker cabinets, they just daub their sticky fingers over everything and cause carnage amongst the ornaments within reach, and good for them, I say.

Recriminations and learning

When the accident's happened and the cleaning-up is done, it's safe to have a few calm words about what caused it – words about paying attention or concentrating a bit more on tea rather than trying to rush to get back to the telly.

And finally ... if by the age of 15 this is still a regular occurrence, *then* you can shout!

If you do reach the stage when a 'crime' has been committed, then you might feel the need to dole out some punishment. This reminds me of the old joke 'Why do people always take their kids to the supermarket to slap them?' and yet, when I see it happen, it breaks my heart. I know opinion is very divided and polarised on the issue of physical punishment (smacking) and you may not agree with my view but here it is anyway.

I'm not a 'hitter', can't see the point. I'm not a saint and there have been the odd times when I have been angry and/or disappointed with the children when they would probably have preferred a slap to break the tension and get back on with real life again – these occasions are rare but I don't hit them because I can't see any positive benefit, in the short, medium or long term, for *anyone* concerned.

If you are the child, it hurts, usually in two ways. First, there's the physical pain and second, the humiliation, which I believe occurs under all circumstances but is clearly the more so in the public arena of the supermarket. This combination can often result in tears, increasing the humiliation; what's more I've seen genuine disappointment on the faces of the 'supermarket parents' if crying hasn't ensued. How bizarre and cruel is that? Of course, kids can be unspeakably horrible, we all know that, but I fail to see how this kind of violent behaviour towards them can teach any lesson they couldn't learn in a better way.

If you're the adult in this situation, you lose too. You have hurt (in two ways) someone who you love very much and you have shown yourself to be unable to convince them to behave in a different way, which is hardly a glowing testament to your intelligence, your maturity or your parenting skills.

Right now, I feel tempted to say that the hitters are exercising an *animal* instinct, a base-level reaction as a way of altering their children's behaviour, but in all honesty I can't recall a single David Attenborough documentary that contained footage of any other *animal* on the planet deliberately inflicting pain on its young as a way of helping it learn. Teaching right and wrong is natural, instilling a sense of discipline in the home essential, violence pointless.

A story about punishment

I have a great friend who tells affectionately of childhood naughtiness that resulted, on occasion, in his dad 'taking his belt off to us'. This was more likely to happen 'if he'd had a few'.

My mate laughingly reassures me that this 'never did me any harm' and I have to say, he is one of the gentlest, kindest, most genuine blokes I have ever known, so I find it hard to argue with that fact. However, the truth is that no one on earth will ever convince me that it did him any *good*.

This kind of story tends to horrify most grown-ups I know, although for many of them there's a spectrum of punishment where this kind of brutality is at the far end but the gentle admonishing slap, or 'love tap' as they like to call it, is OK. I just don't get it; where's the 'love' in that? I'm well aware that if you disagree with my point of view, you will by now be thinking of me as a politically correct, sandaled beardie who should stop interfering with the very proper rights of every parent to give their offspring a good thwack now and again. For me, the plain truth is that you can't love kids too much, so why should that hurt?

I said at the beginning of this chapter that I thought it was important to have a good think about the kind of 'regime' you want to create and explained that it stops you being too reactive. In my own case, I've got nothing written down (that would be sad) but more a voice in my head that tells me what's acceptable and what's not, in different circumstances. I think that if you were to fire scenarios at me, I could tell you with a pretty high degree of accuracy how I'd react. So, think about the continuum between dictatorship and democracy from the last chapter, choose where you want to be on the line and try to be consistent about it. Most importantly of all, communicate it through both words and deeds to the children. Tell them what's open for question, the issues that may be debated and the amount of weight you'll place on their opinions, and make it clear what is not up for discussion. If you're feeling very radical, you might even explain why: 'No, Rupert, you may not bring class A drugs into the house, because they are illegal'.

How to know when you're successful

Once you've set the standards, be prepared for occasional fireworks, where you light the blue touch-paper and retire to a safe distance. Without doubt there will be times when a rebellion breaks out. If they don't question me sometimes, if they don't attempt to get their own way, then I feel like I've failed as a father. Sporadic domestic anarchy can be a very positive force; don't knock it.

17

Show some emotion

It's not a very widespread or popular view but in general I think that blokes are much more emotional than women, we're just not very good at showing it. No, that's not strictly true, we tend only to show emotion within a strict set of rules. If you think that men can't be passionate, go to a local football derby on a Saturday afternoon and watch the behaviour on the terraces.

Fortunately, we're getting better in more *personal* circumstances too and aren't nearly so buttoned up as the last generation, but the picture is still patchy. Contrast these two 'leaving home' stories. I recall a friend of mine telling me about the day *he* left home, his dad stood on the doorstep, hands in pockets, nodded a goodbye and said the immortal words 'Well, I'll be seeing you'. I was a bit luckier. Our company had relocated and a horde of us were moving to another part of the country, in a way I guess I'd been forced into leaving home. At six in the morning on the first Monday one of the other lads came to pick me up in his car and as I left, my dad had tears in his eyes. This, I think, was the first time I ever saw him cry, the first time in 23 years and it had a massive effect on me. He didn't wait quite as long for the second time, as I got another job and returned home within 12 weeks.

Going back another generation, things were even worse. I went to visit Great-Uncle Billy in hospital and knew he was dying (maybe he did too) and although we were never close (only saw each other at Christmas and family get-togethers), before I left, I felt a great sadness and leant over to kiss him goodbye, maybe for the final time. Despite his frail condition he shot across the bed like a whippet, to avoid my advances, and gave me a look which said 'What do you think I am, a homosexual?' Big mistake.

These days you do see much more physical affection between men and it's not unusual for friends to have a warmer-than-once handshake or even a hug. I openly admit that I like it but nonetheless understand that it still makes some blokes uncomfortable.

It's easy to *love* your children but for some of us the legacy of past generations and their stand-off-ishness means that it's not always as easy to show it and although they will probably always know how much you cared, even in the most 'stuffed shirt' of relationships, it's much better if you're able to articulate your feelings. Do your best to show them how much you love them.

Hugs and kisses

When kids are very young, we find it easy to indulge in lots of hugs and kisses irrespective of their gender.

Physical affection is a very fair-minded thing, you both get an equal amount of pleasure out of it. As the years go by, it is clearly easier to maintain this kind of affection with daughters but you need to remember that the kind of conditioning we grew up with, all the more severe in Uncle Billy's day, will inevitably leave its lasting legacy on the current generation of sons, so at some point you can guarantee that they will be less inclined to be kissed, especially, and I emphasise this, *especially in public*. Although I'm still 'allowed' to be affectionate with my son in the confines of our own home, if I ever drop him off at school a kiss goodbye would be considered the height of bad taste. These days we resort to me giving him a brief but robust tousling of his hair before he gets out of the car and I suspect that 'these days' may also be numbered.

With luck, I may get back to some kind of more affectionate contact, once the next phase has passed. Maybe when he's 20 and I'm dropping him off at university, he'll give me a big 'man-hug' as I leave, just so he can whip a twenty quid note out of my back pocket.

I have less, and different, concerns about my daughter. Society allows her to be open and loving in her contact with me, though as she reaches the stage of developing fully into womanhood I guess she'll have to stop sitting on my knee, not because I think it's inappropriate but because she's getting heavy.

words

Gestures and body language can convey an awful lot but there's no replacement for telling your children how you feel about them. I can't quite understand it if dads are reluctant to do this because if you feel strongly about them, why wouldn't you say so? We habitually say 'I love you' whenever we're parting, either in person or on the phone and I think that's a really good thing, but now and again, to prove you're not just saying the words, you need to choose another time to tell them. Sometimes I do this when they're going to bed, I'll tuck them up, look squarely into their eyes and tell them how I feel, but it doesn't always have to have this intensity. It's actually quite good to do it as a throw-away sometimes, so in the middle of having breakfast you could casually drop it into the conversation.

And those 'three little words' aren't the only ones you can use. At the right time you can tell them 'I'm so proud of you', 'You're very special', 'You really make me laugh'. As well as expressing your feelings it builds their self-esteem: praise, praise, praise and then a bit more praise; and don't worry about their becoming big-headed or thinking they're better than they are, that big cruel world outside has a habit of keeping us grounded and all you're doing is redressing the balance of some of the criticism they are bound to face.

If by nature you are a shy person and find it difficult to verbalise your feelings in this way, you can always write it down. As you're not with the children all the time, you could resort to writing a good old-fashioned letter. It's a shame that this art appears to be dying out but letters are extra special precisely for the reason that they are now rather an oddity. It doesn't have to be a schmaltzy love letter either, you can chat away merrily about what you've been doing, plans for the future, your interest in their school life, but finish with something special that tells them how you feel about them.

Email works well too and although it's less formal, it has the benefit of being more spontaneous, plus you can show your thoughtfulness in other ways if you send them a digital photo or a link to a website that you know will interest or amuse them. Re-inforce it with a sign-off that says 'Thinking of you' or something similar.

Secrets

A great way of bonding with another individual is if you share a secret together, something only you know. This can be anything from a secret sign or look through to a bit of shared knowledge. We've got a facial expression nicknamed 'the family look' which implies 'What's all this about?' that we save for social occasions when you're not allowed, by polite protocols, to say it out loud. Similarly, there's a 'Theobald thumb-wave' used for occasions when we can't actually speak to each other, like if they're in the choir at a school concert. A discreet waggle of the thumb says 'Hey look, I'm here' and the reply says 'Yep, I've seen you!' You may not be as facile as us but you can still share some titbit which is special between you, keep secrets innocent and on non-gossipy territory.

one-to-one

I've talked about the things we share as a family but I also mentioned earlier that if there's one thing children love, it's being made a special fuss over. If you get 'one-to-one' time with a child, they can behave completely differently to when they're in the company of other kids, particularly their siblings. Sometimes an eldest child can be much more mature and grown-up if they're not being dragged down to the youngest common denominator of their brothers and sisters. Don't forget that if you've got more than one child, you need to share this special time evenly, not only because you'll be guilty of favouritism if you don't, but also because you get different reactions and responses from each of them. They love being seen as an individual rather than part of a collective pack. Teachers I know confirm this – even the most 'difficult' children can be reached on an individual basis.

It may be that as part of this you have a special secret with each child, which is fine as long as you don't inadvertently let it slip to their siblings; in fact it's better not mentioned at all.

Being there
For all my talk of verbalising your feelings, there are times when actions speak louder than words, for example with your attendance at events that are special to the children. This might be as important as their birthday but could equally well be the school nativity play. Don't use weasel words like 'I'll try to get there if I can'. If you think you can't make it, then say so, at least that way they won't be craning their necks to spot you, only to be disappointed. On the other hand, if you say you definitely will be there, ensure you don't let them down. The feeling of deflation will spoil the whole event for them.

If you've got the pressures of a full-time job, you'll be lucky if you can get to even a handful of these events but by staying in touch with the school and the children's social calendar you can plan ahead and either book a day's holiday or negotiate a few hours off with your boss. Again the golden rule of parity applies: if you have more than one offspring, what could be worse than your always attending one child's special events and never the others'?

Ritual

You might find it hard to make time for all this 'special-ness' and important though it is, you can just as easily make them feel loved by more routine methods. Twice each day there is a natural opportunity for this: first thing in the morning and last thing at night. At the weekend especially you have a chance to savour the time together and can introduce a routine where they pile into bed with you and you have tea and toast together and talk about the day ahead; my sister (whose children are almost grown-up now) used to call this 'the best bit of the day'. In the same way you can make a ritual of bedtime and what could be better than falling asleep with happy contended thoughts of how valued you are? Even if you only spend one minute with each child giving them a cuddle and telling them you love them, it's a great invest-ment in their (and your) emotional well-being.

You might also review the day that's gone, emphasis-ing the good bits and minimising the bad – after all, tomorrow's a whole new opportunity to start again. On the other hand, they might have a favourite story you can read, or a song you sing. I know we have.

Shut up and listen

Children want to know you're interested in them, it makes them feel good. There's not always the time to listen intently to what's happening in their lives but if you never do it, it won't be long before they realise that there's no point in telling you because you just don't care. It's no good getting frustrated if you then ask them 'What happened at school today?' and they reply 'Oh, not much'. Active listening means you can't read the newspaper or watch the match at the same time. You have to look them in the eyes, ask relevant questions and take heed of the answers. It's really good too if you remember what they say and ask them again about the same topic at some later time.

If during this they talk to you about their problems, don't feel compelled to come up with instant answers, especially if the solutions don't fit with their character ('Well if I were you, I'd just punch him on the nose!'). Instead, encourage them to problem-solve in their own way by asking 'What do you think would make things better?' and be supportive of their suggestions if you think they're right. If they come up with an answer that might not be fitting, talk through the implications of it (e.g. 'Punching him on the nose might seem like a good idea but have you seen the size of his dad?'). Being dismissive or suggesting your own method of sorting out the world gives them no opportunity to discover how to deal with issues in their own way.

court them

Think about the ways you might behave if you were in love with a woman and it'll tell you all you need to know to make your children feel wanted. I've already talked about written communication but try putting a secret note under their pillow or, if you get the chance, in their lunchbox for school. It doesn't have to be soppy, a shared joke has the same effect. The comedian Spike Milligan wrote miniature 'fairy' letters for his children, which he would then hide around the house or garden for them to discover. Making them feel special isn't about how much you lavish on them (though this doesn't go amiss now and again), but the attention you give.

Just because they're your kids, there's no reason to take them for granted so try to make a point of showing your affection in different ways that will signal you are thinking about them. If you've listened to their chatter (see above), you can pick up easily what's on their minds and surprise them with your thoughtfulness. This might be something as simple as buying a new kind of 'pop' that they've seen in a TV advert and have commented on 'how cool' it looks. When they show an interest in a particular programme, you could tape a few episodes when they're not with you, which you can sit and watch together or even investigate a few websites on the latest blockbuster movie they're raving about and store them in a separate folder of their favourites. Alternatively, you can take them on a shopping trip to choose (with your guidance!) the new wallpaper or paint for their bedroom. These are just a few ideas but there are hundreds more that will make them know they're special to you.

Tailored games

Inventing your own versions of well-tried favourites is a great idea. One of the easiest is a treasure hunt, great for a wet winter's day when no one feels like venturing out. You can tailor this to their favourite movie character, like James Bond, for example, or pick a theme around the toys they play with most. Dress it up as a 'spy mission', 'crime-fighting' or something equally adventurous. When you get really clever (and when they're old enough), you can make the clues more cryptic or even write them in verse and if you give each of them (and yourself) a character name (maybe even some costumes and props), the whole event turns into an adventure. At the end of the hunt there needs to be some kind of reward (usually chocolate in our house) but for the sake of fairness and so as not to spoil the fun it's better to set each child off on a different course so that the rewards end up even. Egg hunting at Easter is a bit like this but it's best if you get mini-eggs wrapped in different coloured foils, one for each child. This way you'll even find that they collaborate to find each other's chocky.

Freedom of choice

It's not long before children start to form opinions about all sorts of things: what they like to eat; their favourite T-shirt, and so on. So it only seems fair that when you're looking for things to do with them they should be able to have some input. To avoid disasters suggest a *menu* of things that everyone can join in with and be prepared to put yourself out now and again. Do something that may not be your cup of tea but which you know brings immense pleasure to them. If they see you being self-sacrificing on their behalf, they'll know how special they are to you.

If all this makes the relationship with your children sound like one great love affair, then fine because that's what it is. All of us want to be wanted, want to be loved, cherished, adored and to know that someone cares, someone who'll always be there for us, without judgement, prejudice or conditions. For them you can be that person. What could make any child happier?

SECTION V

THE FUTURE (ABOUT YOU)

18

Girls, girls, girls

Whether you have decided to stay steadfastly single or crave curvaceous company, you still need to think seriously and consciously about the issue of women (in fact there are times when I think of little else). The reason is that your new relationships with the opposite sex will have an effect on how you relate to your children. Because, whether you like it or not, the pair-bonding that resulted in your lovely offspring being born is part of life and there are issues to deal with whether or not you choose to 'go there again'.

Flying solo

I'll deal with being single first, simply because, believe me, it's simpler – sorry, I forgot who I was talking to for a minute. I don't need to tell you that, do I? Staying single, I mean consciously deciding to, rather than not being able to 'get off with a lady' is an option I've always seen as attractive, at least for a while. If you're a bit shell-shocked after your split, it's really beneficial to give yourself a bit of time and space to decide what you want next. Tempting though it is to prove (to yourself) that you're still attractive, it's a dangerous game to play if you're on the rebound.

If you can take a break instead and reflect on what went wrong last time, including what you could have done differently, this just might stop you from making the same mistakes again; there are no guarantees here but it's worth a try. Think also about the kind of person you are: would you be happy to cope alone, not just with your own needs, but with child care too?

Finally, and maybe most importantly, what sort of a state are the kids in? Do they seem to be picking themselves up and getting on with it or is their behaviour volatile and unpredictable, have they articulated their feelings, do you know their hopes and fears? This last point is particularly important, as introducing a new girlfriend to them before they're ready could end in disaster.

Some people find that being long-term single is a miserable state of affairs, though I've always been OK with it. Of course, there will inevitably be things you miss about being in a relationship, but certainly in the early days it's worth remembering that the process of getting control and freedom back in your life was a painful and probably costly one. You may not be in too much of a rush to throw that away. It's also a rather chilling fact that second marriages have a higher failure rate than first ones, so statistically you are on even shakier ground than last time.

Pair-bonding

However, the time may come when you are ready once more to dip your toe in the water and you'll soon realise that things have changed considerably since you last played the dating game. People who have been out of circulation for a bit should come with a health warning so that unwary new partners know what they're letting themselves in for. There are some classic first-date turn-offs that you should avoid, including talking in great detail about your split-up, all the things that were wrong with your marriage or an endless whinge about child-care issues. That's not to deny that these are significant things in your life right now but you don't need to share them all at once, and a degree of humility about how it takes two to make a marriage and two to break it won't go amiss.

The dating game (again!)

So, you're footloose again but just where does a chap go, what does he do if once more in the pursuit of a fair maiden? You could, if you were very romantic, leave it to fate, but be warned, it might be a long wait. Sometimes fate needs a little push.

Old wives' tales include the one about the likelihood of meeting a new life partner in the supermarket; old divorcees' tales say this is complete bollocks. All that stuff about being able to find true love in the aisles of your local Tesco: utter rubbish. The theory goes like this: all you have to do is spot the woman you desire, go up and accidentally-on-purpose bump trolleys, then start up a conversation that culminates in an invitation to dinner and ends with the lights dimming and ...

Unless women are equally deranged in their thinking, you'll find it unlikely that the fairer sex are doing anything other than shopping for groceries, a process that is unpleasant yet necessary. With this in mind, she'll be trying to complete the task in as short a time and with as little hassle as possible. The bumping-trolleys thing is likely, at best, to result in a stony stare or at worst in a warning of 'Can't you watch where you're going?', often from the Neanderthal-looking bloke you've failed to notice but who is quite clearly the other half (or possibly even two-thirds) of your chosen belle. Even if you do strike it lucky, what are you going to use as an opener? 'Oh, I'm so sorry, I wasn't looking where I was going because I was distracted by the enormous amount of lard you're buying'.

Alternatively, there are a number of high-tech routes to romance on the Internet, the first of which involves going back over old ground by digging up a treasure from the past. Friends Reunited and similar websites have been hugely successful in linking up old chums from school-days with the added bonus that we can now all do a bit of online stalking and find out what ex-girlfriends are doing. (Oh, grow up and stop feeling guilty – do you suppose for a minute they're not doing the same?) It would be lovely to think that this is a victimless crime but the plain truth is that for either sex there are times when we can't resist the urge to see how the other party has turned out, and although there are no reliable statistics, there is a lot of anecdotal evidence to suggest that lots of old flames are rekindled and affairs restarted. Well now, that's all fine and dandy, but just because you once went out together is no recipe for long-term success now, in fact the odds are against you simply because you not only dated for a while but also found a reason to stop doing so and maybe it won't take you long to remember what that was. Sometimes it's much better to let sleeping dogs lie.

Your second Internet option involves the opportunity to meet tons of new women – it's online dating. I know you're well used to that 'I have a friend who ...' approach which really means 'It's me but I'm too ashamed to admit it', but honestly, I really *do* have a friend who has done some Internet dating and I've watched him go online and start 'chatting up' women. For me this is like going to the circus to see the man put his head in the lion's mouth: fascinating to watch, to the point where I simply cannot turn away, and yet I would no more venture in there with him than fly to the Moon.

It's not that I think there's anything wrong with online dating services. In fact my logical side tells me it the most sensible way of meeting a suitable match and offers a safe (if done correctly) way of vetting a host of potential partners. Similarly, it allows both sexes the opportunity to browse the shelves without feeling the need to make a purchase. Pretty sensible and very grown-up all round; it's just that the romantic in me kicks against the whole idea of a cyber-match.

I am warming to this theme of modern methods though and the latest of these is speed dating where you condense all the opening flirtatious exchanges of a normal first-meeting into three minutes and repeat the exercise up to 30 times in one night. It's a kind of cattle market in a microwave. You'll have just enough time to say that you're some saddo single daddo on the prowl for a bit of new action, 30 times, which should be sufficient to have every woman in the room heading in the opposite direction. If any of them look vaguely interested, then I would suggest that if you have a pet rabbit now is the time to think about investing in extra hutch security.

If you really are shy and sensitive, in touch with your feminine side, not afraid to express your emotions and count shopping and chocolate among your hobbies, then most women will find *something* attractive about you. However, if you use this as your emotional CV at speed dating, they will find the fact that you are lying a less attractive trait.

All this new-fangled stuff sounds fine for a laugh but if you're serious about finding a new girlfriend, then it's hard to beat the tried and tested methods of your youth. Going out, being sociable, having a few drinks and some laughs sound like a great way of meeting women and quite frankly for some blokes it is. I have to confess my pathological fear of rejection has tended to make this a rather horrific experience for me in the past but if you've got a good line in chat, don't look half bad and are not afraid of the occasional 'slap off', then good luck to you.

You do have to remember that over time the venues change. Everything about them changes – music, the fashion, the drinks and, unless you really are young and trendy, you are very unlikely to look so just by virtue of setting foot in the place, so choose carefully and if possible go with a still-single mate who knows the form.

If night-clubbing is not your scene, then something else probably is, so actively seek out some social activity that puts you in touch with like-minded people. It might mean your joining a local photography or climbing club, or maybe a theatre group or badminton class, it doesn't matter as long as it gets you out and about. The only groups I am highly suspicious of are singles clubs as I get the feeling that most people who join are desperately seeking a lifestyle that is no longer single, with the emphasis here on the desperation.

The complexities of new relationships

However you choose to meet someone and whenever it comes about, it won't be anything like it was before you were married/attached with kids. The key thing to remember is that being a dad is a different scenario from before because now you've got 'baggage', baggage that's fragile, so remember to 'handle with care'. Just as significantly, your own status has changed as you have become a father. With this comes the inevitable responsibility of trying to balance the relationships in your life. A new girlfriend might make the children feel more secure, or alternatively threatened, if they feel she is taking all your attention. It's not likely to be an easy ride for her either, when she took you on she maybe hadn't accounted for the fact that it was buy one get one (or more) free at the relationship-mart. If you're going to pull this trick off, you need to do a lot of listening and talking so that everyone concerned knows what's going on and the feelings that are around. However it's going, it's probably best not to rush things; everyone needs a chance to re-adjust to this new set of circumstances. This might all sound a bit heavy, like the next girl you meet you're going to instantly propose to, but even with fairly relaxed and casual relationships, all concerned will want to know where they stand.

You may also find once you're 'back on the market' that the women you meet have children too but, of course, it's much more likely that they will live with her for most of the time. Now things are really complicated as it's no longer about a relationship between the two of you, it's a matrix arrangement of different liaisons, some of which might work well and others less so.

It would be really stupid of me not to recognise the fact that there is a mating game and during the early stages in particular none of us is 100% truthful for 100% of the time. We're usually busy trying to put the best gloss on ourselves and pretending that we never have, don't now and never will fart.

But aside from the trivia of our bodily functions now is not the time to start messing with other people's emotions: your new girlfriend, her children, your children, it's just too complex for you to bugger about with. Try instead from the start to be an Honest John and be clear about what you want and expect from a relationship. Recognise too, up front, that the road ahead is far more complicated now that children are involved. It's much better this way than to just drift and turn out to be a cad and a scoundrel.

19

The long and winding road

Years ago, I sent off to the BBC for a booklet called *How to be happy*, which accompanied the 'QED' documentary of the same name; it just seemed too good an opportunity to miss. I've still got it somewhere and just thinking about it makes me laugh. That's not quite what they intended of course, what the programme did was outline some scientific theories about how to increase your happiness quotient. In fact if they'd called it by some snappy name like HQ (as in IQ or EQ), they would have probably made a mint out of it.

In the documentary, they took a couple of saddos (they literally were sad people, I'm not being rude), put them through the 'happiness process', which from what I remember involved spending a lot of time looking in the mirror chanting the mantra 'I aaaaammmm haaa-peeeeee!', then measuring how happy they were at the end.

My marvellous booklet outlined how you might do this in the safety of your own home but somehow I never got round to it. I just couldn't bring myself to believe that happiness was based on some scientific formula and that if you mixed the ingredients together in the test-tube of your existence, you would be miraculously transformed from solid to gas (laughing gas that is) overnight. Instead, I've thought quite a lot about what makes me happy, what makes all of us happy, what happiness is and, because I think that your happiness as a single dad is very much linked to the happiness of your children, I've set out below my conclusions.

I think that some of this could be to do with whether we're born happy or not. Could it be that happiness is genetic? If we have miserable parents does it follow that we will be miserable too? Can we introduce 'environmental' factors into our lives which might make us happier?

If you accept my entirely non-scientific thesis that we have a natural capacity to be happy, then no matter where we are on the happiness scale, it seems to me that there are two things we can do. First, we can make the best of what we've got and, second, we can make the most of what we've *got left*. For most of us, I guess it occurs to us when someone we know dies, especially if it's someone from our peer group, our age, that we're not here forever. Under these circumstances we tend to resolve to make more of every day of our lives from then on. It's a pity we don't seem to able to sustain it in the long term.

If you can truly embrace the proper ethos of living each day a little more appreciatively, then I think you're on the route to being happier. I don't want to overplay the morbid bit but look at it this way, we all aspire to dying happy and as we don't know when that day is, the only way to achieve this is to try and be happy *every* day. It's a hell of a way of beating the system.

I'm also aware of many parents saying to me that once you've had children the time just goes, it speeds past faster than any other stage in your life. You know that being pedantic really isn't my thing but I would like to point out that every minute is exactly the same length as the last; time doesn't really speed up. If I just put my soap box to one side for a moment, I will be the first to admit that it *seems* to go quicker and I can only suppose that this is because the rapid development of children, from screaming blob to whingeing teenager, gives us a yardstick to measure the passage of time.

I'll always remember my sister saying to me 'Savour every moment, before you know it, they're gone', this was made all the more poignant by the traipsing through of her teenage son, grunting, belching and raiding the fridge in one seamless pass.

Don't dwell on this too much but if you keep in the back of your mind that 'Oh my God, we're all going to die', then the smell of baby sick is the mere twinkling of an eye when measured against the sands of time and the gratitude you feel because you're alive. It might just make you wake every morning and say out loud 'It's a beautiful day!'

When it comes to making the best of what we're born with, our 'happiness potential' if you like, it's a good idea now and again to stop and consider the things that are important. Here are some of mine:

- *me*

- *the children*

- *my family (mum, dad, brother, sister)*

- *friends*

- *social life*

- *fitness*

- *well-being*

- *health*

- *sex*

- *money*

- *creativity*

- *life experiences*

- *laughter*

- *debate*

- *knowledge*

- *worldliness*

- *work*

- *self-esteem.*

It's not definitive, just the things that immediately occurred to me, and what's more it isn't necessarily in order of significance, but overall it's not a bad summary. Stop and think about your own list, even write it down and mark each item out of ten. Nought means you're thoroughly dissatisfied with the state of that aspect of life, ten means you've got it sorted. Then resolve to be happier by maximising the things that are good and marginalising the bad bits.

⊚⊚⊚⊚

20

Final thoughts

As I draw this book to its conclusion, I have some confessions to make, the first of which is that this is far more personal than I intended it to be. When I set about the task of writing the book, I thought that I'd be able to keep the subject matter at arm's length from where I and my children are, but have found through the process that this is impossible. Paradoxically I think this has made the text much richer as I have shared the real experiences of coping with single fatherhood but I recognise that there may be some passages that friends, family, the children and their mother would have rather I hadn't written and if that is the case then I apologise. By contrast, I hope *you* have found its realism enjoyable, authentic and relevant in parts to the way you are living your life and coping with your circumstances. I'd like to think that the latter justifies the former.

It's equally true that I agonised over the title as it felt as if I were just setting myself up for a fall. Of course, I don't think I'm a great dad, it's something I aspire to and some days it works better than others. As they say, every dad has his day. However, if I'm really honest, it doesn't matter a toss what I think because the ultimate judge of how 'great' or otherwise I am rests not with me but with the two children I have fathered. Somehow the laws of nature tend to lean in our favour: you can be much less than your potential and children still have a way of finding the good things in you, but for me that's not enough to make me sleep easy at night, I have to keep trying, I have to strive to understand what works and what doesn't and attempt to get it right more of the time than I don't.

I am also acutely aware of the short time that we perform our intensive fatherhood duties for. Naturally they will always be around in adult life to 'tap you up' for a few quid – it's nature's way of reminding you that you have kids – but the bit between doing everything for them and their needing you for nothing is so short and it passes in such a blur that the chances are you'll not even notice when they stopped calling you daddy and shortened it to dad. That's just the first of many signs.

Finally, I found it difficult to decide whether or not to add the piece of prose at the end of this chapter which I wrote when we were on holiday. This is partly because it's very personal but also because I think there is a very thin line between its being poetic or naff. In the end I chose to include it for the simple reason that as single dads we all have crap days when we wonder not only *how* we're doing but *why* we're doing it and when that happens I draw solace from the fact that my children are the most special thing in the world to me and every now and then the sheer joy of them bubbles to the surface and leaves me, as it did when I wrote this, feeling inspired, humbled and happy beyond belief. So here goes, this is what I wrote on one of those very special days.

Tuesday 24 February 2004

Today was a day with a very special moment.

We are three-quarters of the way through a fortnight's holiday in Florida.

We? Me and my family; me and my two great children. For these two weeks of the year we are everything to each other – it is just us three – there is nothing else to intrude and nothing of any real importance beyond us enjoying our time together.

It would be easy to dismiss this as 'not real life' because back home we all have other things to think about; the day-to-day concerns of work or school, earning enough to pay the bills or getting the homework done on time, but maybe it is those fifty weeks of the year that are unreal and that these two are the way it's meant to be.

That said, I've explained my theory about happiness to the children before, saying 'We all need sad times to know what happy times are', one is in contrast to the other, it helps you measure it, maybe we need the fifty to help us measure the two.

So, we've thrashed the living daylights out of all Universal Studios can offer us. We've spun webs with Spiderman, duelled with dragons, tackled Jaws, escaped an earthquake and arrived home before we set off on several occasions thanks to the 'Back to the Future' ride. We knocked 'em down, one ride after another, Nancy as intrepid as ever, Ben rising to the challenge and overcoming his anxieties in a way that made me proud inside.

Perhaps the toughest storm to weather came today, it was a real storm, real weather. The Florida sunshine deserted us so we donned our plastic ponchos and squelched from attraction to attraction, grateful for an indoor queue to shelter from the thunderstorms.

Eventually, we arrived at the last of the day, The Twister; some unknown re-enactment of the terrors of a tornado lay ahead of us. We stood, squashed into yet another pre-show warm-up, the collected raindrops trickling down our blue plastic protection and forming puddles around our feet, or worse still, soaking through our shoes and socks.

Two dimly-lit movie screens on the far wall provided the only light, waiting to burst into life with some

disastrous news of a system malfunction and a final
warning to 'Get out while we still can!'

Then, in the middle of all this, it happens, the very
special moment. I take one hand of each of my
children in mine. Their fingers wrap around me – no
longer baby or toddler hands (why did that all pass
so quickly?) but child hands, not-that-much-longer-
child hands. These are hands that I know will so
soon be grown-up, full size and independent and
right there, right then, I know I have to savour the
moment.

So, I do – I look at the blank screens, I feel the cool,
rain-drenched, slightly clammy little hands, I feel
them holding me nervously, because it is dark and
none of us knows what is coming. I feel in them
both the anxiety of the unknown and the surety that
everything will be OK because I am there.

I feel the responsibility of making sure that everything
is OK and though I know that this palpable
dependence will soon be gone, I will always and
forever want to make everything OK for them.

In that fleeting moment I am proud
and happy
and aware
and humble
and privileged
and uplifted.

What wonderful children – What a wonderful life –
How lucky I am.

Not all days are like that but one fact is irrefutable: every single day I am their dad, it's my job, it doesn't earn me any money, I'll never get promoted, in the end I'll be redundant (or virtually), the pension is non-existent and the hours are non-negotiable, but for all that it's the best job I've ever had, the best job anyone can ever have.

End note

When all's said and done I've reached one cast-iron conclusion about parenting which is so obvious in its simplicity as to be hardly worth stating. None of the collected knowledge of past generations, none of the sound down-to-earth advice of trusted friends, nor any of the assembled thoughts in these pages can come close to it. In fact I am drawn to reflect that the only reason we seek other sources to supplement our existing skills is that our lives are so complex and intricate, the expectations of us so great and the challenges so immense that we often feel the need to rely on something outside ourselves.

And yet, if you strip away everything else, your single-dad skills are based on instinct, the greatest, strongest and most unmovable of which is to love your kids. Do that. Show them and tell them that and you will, in their eyes, be the Greatest Dad in the World.

Good Luck.

Notes

Notes

Notes

Notes

Notes